About Island Press

Island Press is the only nonprofit organization in the United States whose principal purpose is the publication of books on environmental issues and natural resource management. We provide solutions-oriented information to professionals, public officials, business and community leaders, and concerned citizens who are shaping responses to environmental problems.

In 2000, Island Press celebrates its sixteenth anniversary as the leading provider of timely and practical books that take a multidisciplinary approach to critical environmental concerns. Our growing list of titles reflects our commitment to bringing the best of an expanding body of literature to the environmental community throughout North America and the world.

Support for Island Press is provided by The Jenifer Altman Foundation, The Bullitt Foundation, The Mary Flagler Cary Charitable Trust, The Nathan Cummings Foundation, The Geraldine R. Dodge Foundation, The Charles Engelhard Foundation, The Ford Foundation, The German Marshall Fund of the United States, The George Gund Foundation, The Vira I. Heinz Endowment, The William and Flora Hewlett Foundation, The W. Alton Jones Foundation, The John D. and Catherine T. MacArthur Foundation, The Andrew W. Mellon Foundation, The Charles Stewart Mott Foundation, The Curtis and Edith Munson Foundation, The National Fish and Wildlife Foundation, The New-Land Foundation, The Oak Foundation, The Overbrook Foundation, The David and Lucile Packard Foundation, The Pew Charitable Trusts, The Rockefeller Brothers Fund, Rockefeller Financial Services, The Winslow Foundation, and individual donors

Nature
and the
Marketplace

Nature
and the
Marketplace

Capturing the Value of Ecosystem Services

Geoffrey Heal

ISLAND PRESS

Washington, D.C. • Covelo, California

ISLAND PRESS is a trademark of the Center for Resource Economics.

Library of Congress Cataloging-in-Publication Data

Heal, G. M.
  Nature and the marketplace : capturing the value of ecosystem services
/ Geoffrey Heal.
      p. cm.
Includes bibliographical references and index.
    ISBN 1-55963-795-1 (acid-free) — ISBN 1-55963-796-X (pbk. :
acid-free)
    1. Green marketing. 2. Product management—Environmental aspects. 3.
Social responsibility of business. I. Title.
    HF5413 .H42 2000
    658.8—dc21
                                    00-010446

Printed on recycled, acid-free paper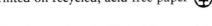

Manufactured in the United States of America
10 9 8 7 6 5 4 3 2 1

Contents

Preface

The natural environment provides the infrastructure on which human societies are built. But human actions are now affecting these foundations in quite unprecedented ways. Our impacts are generally a result of economic activities: growing food, running vehicles, heating and cooling buildings. So as environmental resources become ever more depleted and damaged, we have to face a critical question: How can we make sure that we do not continue to damage the natural foundations of our societies while earning our living? How can we make our economic activities compatible with our ecological foundations?

To date humanity has been remarkably fortunate in this respect. We have not had to invest in maintaining the natural infrastructure of our societies. It has been self-repairing. But the more of us there are and the more lavishly a few of us live, the more demands we place on our planetary home. We may be starting to exceed its capacity and to subject it to substantial wear and tear. If this is indeed happening—and many scientists believe this to be the case—then our years of maintenance- and rent-free living may come to an end. There is no planetary landlord to whom we will have to pay rent, but there may be planetary repair and maintenance bills, the costs of keeping our basic systems intact and functioning well.

It is these planetary repair bills that are the concern of this book: the economic issues raised by the impact of human activity on ecosystem services and on the global cycles controlled by them. To what extent can our current economic institutions and policies manage these impacts appropriately? Will our institutions ensure that the bills are not excessive and are paid when needed so that our natural infrastructure continues to deliver the services on which we depend?

The exploration of these questions can give us an important new perspective on environmental conservation: it can be seen as a global form of household maintenance, as a form of investment in maintaining key aspects of our infrastructure. It is the global equivalent of housekeeping: it is earthkeeping.

My goal in writing this book is to share a vision of how humans can manage their interactions with the natural environment on which their prosperity and well-being are ultimately based. I examine how natural systems and processes benefit human societies and seek to identify the economic policies and institutions needed to maintain their integrity.

I approach these issues strictly from an economic and business perspective, as an economist with an interest in the environment, not as an environmentalist or environmental scientist. I teach at a business school, have started and run companies, and regularly work for large corporations. My perspective on environmental issues contains a pragmatic and utilitarian element, which makes it rather unemotional relative to much of what is written. There certainly is a role for emotions when we think about such issues as the extinction of species and the loss of beautiful environments. I claim no particular expertise in leading a discussion of such issues. What I bring to the table is experience in looking at cause and effect in economic systems and in understanding how business opportunities and incentives create prosperity, which is where this book focuses.

To a very real extent, the problems we face lie at the interface between economics and ecology. And so may their solutions. The management of our interaction with the natural foundations of our societies need not and indeed must not be economically restrictive. There is no doubt that we must change many of the ways in which we interact economically with nature; however, in many if not all cases this can be done with economic gain rather than loss. The old maxim "Necessity is the mother of invention" suggests a common-sense, pragmatic approach: environmental problems can create business opportunities.

Sound economics and sound ecology are not mutually exclusive. In fact, they have a semantic root and much in the way of intellectual structure in common. Their common beginning, *eco,* derives from *oikos,* the Greek word for "housekeeping." In fact, the Greek origins of *economics* denote "human housekeeping," while those of *ecology* denote "nature's housekeeping." Maintaining a sharp distinction between them may have once made sense, but now human activity is driving many changes in nature; humans have inadvertently become one of the main drivers of planetary change. Consequently the distinction between human and nature's housekeeping is no longer as sharp as it once was. We need to think about "earthkeeping," in the sense of considering our impacts on the planet as a whole, not just on our own households.

Currently we have no explicit mechanisms for managing and mitigating the impact of economic activity on our natural foundations. I analyze the possibility of extending the scope of our main economic institution, the market mechanism, to this area. There is real potential here, although this is certainly not a panacea. The market mechanism is an extraordinarily sophisticated and versatile social institution: it cannot solve all economic problems, but when it works it does so well and simply and elegantly. It creates no fuss and little bureaucracy, and is essentially self-managing. There are alternatives when needed, but when it can be used, the market is the mechanism of choice. Regulatory mechanisms have been widely used but are usually less efficient and less acceptable politically than the market. I explore this concept in several chapters.

My central argument is that markets can be valuable tools in mitigating our impacts on the natural systems that provide infrastructure to our societies. To some in the environmental movement, however, the market has been seen as the problem, not the solution. And certainly economic activity drives much damage to the environment. But this is not the same as saying that the market drives damage to the environment. Think of the former Soviet Union, a society whose economic organization was based on a complete rejection of the market. Its economic activity was far less in extent than that of the United States, and far less successful in every way—which is the main reason it is no longer with us. Yet its environmental impacts were far more negative. We have to distinguish between physical economic activity—making and distributing food, transportation services, and so forth—and the social institutions within which economic activity is conducted, which may be market or nonmarket or a shade in between. Almost certainly, nonmarket economic activity has been more damaging to the environment than equivalent activity organized through the market. Markets are tools that we can use to solve certain economic problems. To date we have used them very effectively to manage financial risks—this is the role of stock markets and associate derivative markets. We have also used them well to manage the development of the high-technology sector. We have not yet really tried to use them for environmental purposes.

The preservation of the natural environment matters to us all and affects us all. It can only be achieved if a majority of us understand the need for it. So the discussions here, while they represent original research and analysis, are intended to be accessible to a broader group than those who have a professional involvement in economics or ecology. I hope in this manner to communicate with students in a variety of disciplines and with the educated public outside of my professional community.

As an economist rather than ecologist I have had to draw on the expertise of colleagues in ecology to understand the environmental science aspects of the subject. In this I have been remarkably fortunate: several of the leading scholars in that field have been generous with their time and patience in educating me. In particular, this book would never have been written without Gretchen Daily, whose volume *Nature's Services: Societal Dependence on Natural Ecosystems* (1997) attracted my interest in the ecosystem services paradigm. Gretchen has also been incredibly helpful in educating me on issues in ecology and explaining her extremely acute vision of the interface between our two disciplines. David Tilman played a crucial role in focusing my attention on the importance of biodiversity and helping me understand biodiversity from an economic perspective. Paul

Ehrlich has been a tremendous help, an encyclopedic source of biological knowledge and a constructive thinker about the economics-ecology interface.[1] Gretchen Daily, Paul Ehrlich, and Roz Naylor kindly commented in detail on the manuscript. All have been immensely supportive at the personal level, encouraging me to pursue my interest in this unconventional approach. I am also grateful to the Center for Environmental Science and Policy at Stanford University, which acted as my host while I wrote this book. Wally Falcon and Don Kennedy, codirectors of the center, were unfailingly supportive and encouraging. Last but most definitely not least, Fran Haselsteiner, acting as editor on behalf of Island Press, has contributed immeasurably to the improvement of the original manuscript, enhancing the clarity and sharpness of the exposition and the argument in many places.

There follow nine chapters and a concluding chapter. The first chapter introduces readers to the infrastructure that natural systems provide human societies and the ways in which we use and depend on that infrastructure. It also reminds us of how we are affecting that infrastructure and possibly destroying some of its value to us. Chapter 2 presents some basic ideas about how a market economy operates, about how the invisible hand of the market and the price mechanism lead, under certain conditions, to the efficient use of society's resources. It focuses particularly on the market in an environmental context. Later chapters apply these ideas about the functioning of a market economy to the services provided by the natural environment: Can we establish markets in the services that the environment provides to human societies?

Chapters 3, 4, and 5 focus on cases where there appears to be a real chance of using market forces to provide incentives for conserving the environment—watersheds, ecotourism, and carbon sequestration. These are important cases; implementing the ideas presented in these chapters could have a far-reaching impact on the preservation of important aspects of the environment.

---

1. Paul's book *A World of Wounds: Ecologists and the Human Dilemma* (1997) is a stimulating and earlier attempt to link our two subjects from the perspective of someone on the other side of the fence.

Chapter 6 looks at a broader range of services provided by the environment. It reviews the whole of biodiversity from an economic perspective: What kind of commodity is it, and what services does it provide, beyond those analyzed in Chapters 3, 4, and 5? Biodiversity can be seen as something that enhances the robustness and productivity of natural and agricultural ecosystems, provides insurance against some of the most serious threats to human food supplies, and provides knowledge of interesting and potentially useful molecular structures. The systems whose robustness it enhances include those that provide us with water and oxygen. It is, in short, important economically. In spite of this, it will be difficult to rely entirely on markets directly for the conservation of many important aspects of biodiversity, largely because of what are in essence issues involving intellectual property rights. This is particularly true of the productivity-, knowledge-, and insurance-enhancing roles of biodiversity.

To understand the strengths and weaknesses of the market mechanism, we need to understand that even if a good is of great economic importance, a market may not realize a value for the good that corresponds to this importance. This is the subject of Chapter 7, on valuation. It asks how market economies value commodities, and what is the connection between market values and importance in a more biological and intuitive sense. Understanding the diamond-water paradox is central here—why do markets value diamonds above water when they are clearly less important? Chapter 8 then looks into a range of policy options other than the market, including the creation of markets for the right to pollute and the introduction of markets into the operation of the Endangered Species Act through mitigation-banking provisions. A market for the right to pollute was introduced in the United States for sulfur dioxide by the 1990 Clean Air Act and is proposed for global emissions of carbon dioxide by the Kyoto Protocol.

Chapter 9 is a move in a rather different direction. It is devoted to an analysis of the fashionable and topical concept of sustainability and sustainable economic development. In this chapter I try to tie the earlier discussion of markets and their potential to issues related to the passage of time and to equity between generations. One of the main concerns of many who worry about our impact on the environment is that we are somehow impoverishing our successors, our children and grandchildren. In Chapter 9 I ask how these issues emerge in a market economy and whether such concerns are well founded.

If we were able to realize the potential of market forces and economic incentives in the areas of ecotourism, watersheds, and forests, the global impact would be truly far-reaching. We would revolutionize human interactions with our planet, taking a tremendous step toward the conservation of vital planetary systems. We would contribute to improving human health, stabilizing carbon and hydrological cycles, and conserving biodiversity. The importance of setting up positive economic incentives for conservation simply cannot be overemphasized. It is up to those of us who want these systems to be conserved to ensure that local populations can earn an income from them without destroying them. As I will show, there are many cases in which this is possible. If the economic incentives are right, there will be less conflict between conservation and economic progress. A growing quality of life for the human population will be compatible with a secure place on Earth for the species that share our world with us. But for this to happen we need practical and compelling solutions, which in some cases the market can offer.

Geoffrey Heal
April 2000

Chapter 1

Infrastructure and Earthkeeping

The quality of our lives—indeed, even our existence—depends on the functioning of natural systems. Natural systems supply air, water, and food. They keep the climate habitable—not too hot or cold, not too wet or dry. They protect us from threats—both animate, such as crop-attacking insects, and inanimate, such as ultraviolet radiation. They cleanse the environment of wastes.

To our ancestors the importance of these systems was self-evident. They were, literally, deified. Each was associated with a god, like the wind god or the sun god or the god of lakes and rivers or the goddess of fertility. They were forces that exacted immediate costs in human suffering.

As we have developed more ways to mitigate the inhospitable aspects of life on Earth, we have become less aware of the environment's importance. To a population brought up on the Promethean achievements of human technologies and for whom space travel, nuclear power, and genetic engineering are no longer novel, nature only infrequently appears powerful. Our technologies seem to insulate us from the natural world. It appears that nature has always been there for us, and that it always will.

Biologists refer to the life-supporting and life-enhancing services of natural ecosystems as "ecosystem services." In an influential

1

recent book, *Nature's Services: Societal Dependence on Natural Ecosystems* (1997), Gretchen Daily provides this definition:

> Natural ecosystems perform critical life-support services, upon which the well-being of all societies depends. These include:
>
> - purification of air and water
> - mitigation of droughts and floods
> - generation and preservation of soils and renewal of their fertility
> - detoxification and decomposition of wastes
> - pollination of crops and natural vegetation
> - dispersal of seeds
> - cycling and movement of nutrients
> - control of the vast majority of potential agricultural pests
> - maintenance of biodiversity
> - protection of coastal shores from erosion by waves
> - protection from the sun's harmful ultraviolet rays
> - stabilization of the climate
> - moderation of weather extremes and their impacts
> - provision of aesthetic beauty and intellectual stimulation that lift the human spirit.

In more prosaic, economic terms, natural ecosystems provide critical infrastructure for human societies. The word *infrastructure* usually conveys images of essential built systems: drainage, sewage, electric power, gas, telephone systems, roads, bridges, and many other complex systems on which our lifestyle depends. Like natural systems, we tend to take these for granted—at least those of us in countries where they function well do. We appreciate their importance when we go to countries where they work erratically. We also come to realize their importance when we lose them, as in the aftermath of a disaster such as an earthquake or a serious storm. It is symptomatic of their importance that the first task after such a disaster is always the reconstruction of whatever basic infrastructure has been destroyed. If a region of the United States or another industrialized country is without any of these basic infrastructure systems for any length of time, this is headline news.

Natural ecosystems are the essential, low-level infrastructure upon which human activities and built systems rest. Fortunately they seem to be exceptionally robust so that to date we have little experience of doing without them. Natural ecosystems provide us with services that in many ways resemble those provided by conventional utilities. Think of the services provided by a house, many of which rely upon and extend those provided by utilities. A house provides local climate-control services, preventing us from being too hot or cold and controlling moisture and wind. In providing these services it draws on outside utilities and on its own structure. In heating or cooling it uses electricity or gas, and in keeping out wind and rain it uses its own structure. It may contain air purification systems. A house provides drainage and waste disposal services via its connections to local utilities or through its own disposal systems. It should ideally be a beautiful and cheerful place, one where we enjoy being and which provides spiritual uplift. It supplies us with drinking water, and with energy via electric power. It protects us from insects and other predators.

If we think about this list and the list given by Daily, we can see many parallels between them. In this sense it really is appropriate to think of the Earth and its natural systems as a home for humanity. It is not just a home in the obvious physical sense of the place where we reside, but also a home in the more basic sense of a place that provides us with much of what we need to be comfortable, to be secure, and to prosper. This is the real sense of the word *home*.

Natural systems provide all of these services, on a far larger scale, of course. They provide even more: a key group of natural services relate to the provision of food. These include pollination, seed dispersal, nutrient cycling, control of soil fertility, and pest control. Despite all the technology we bring to bear on our habitats, we cannot duplicate this: we cannot create environments in which food can be produced from its basic chemical constituents. A 1999 report on the importance of biodiversity in agriculture (Council for Agricultural Science and Technology) made this point well:

> Humans don't produce food. Other species produce it for us. The essence of agriculture is the harnessing of numerous species of plants and animals for human benefit.

Many of the advances in agriculture have come from the discovery of new crops and from genetic refinements in these crops.

Our homes provide several other services that are based on and extend those provided by natural systems. For example, a good home with no leaks controls the climate locally: it keeps its occupants warm, dry, and out of the wind. But it can only do this provided the external environment is within certain limits; if external winds rise to hurricane intensity, with corresponding levels of rainfall, most houses will no longer keep us warm and dry. If the external temperature were to rise to 120 degrees Fahrenheit or fall to 20 degrees below zero, most houses would be inadequate for keeping their inhabitants comfortable. If the climate were to change so that hurricanes or extreme temperatures were more common, much of our human-made infrastructure would be quite inadequate and would no longer perform its function of keeping us comfortable and secure.

To make the same point in a different context, a very basic requirement for any home is that it provide drinkable water. Home plumbing systems are linked to public water-supply systems that bring water from reservoirs or aquifers. If the climate were to change so that reservoirs did not refill and aquifers did not replenish, then again our own contribution to infrastructure would be valueless. So the infrastructure systems that we build depend on natural infrastructure. Indeed, the natural infrastructure is assumed. Without functioning climate systems and hydrological cycles, our built systems would be inadequate for their tasks.

Planetary Impacts of Human Activity

The scale of the human endeavor has grown so large that it is affecting even basic planetary systems that have been in existence for hundreds of millions of years. These are systems that have created the environment in which we evolved and upon which we depend in myriad ways. Protecting the environment at this level has only recently become a goal pursued by environmental policy. Going forward, it will be one of the main goals. The Montreal Protocol on

Substances That Deplete the Ozone Layer and the Kyoto Protocol of the United Nations Framework Convention on Climate Change (Benedick 1998) are examples of recent or emerging policy measures directed at maintaining the integrity of global systems. Both address phenomena that could change global environmental systems central in supporting life on Earth.

What are these global systems upon which we depend and that we are now compromising? Typically they are complex interactions between biological, geological, and chemical systems. According to Daily (1997), the ecosystem services we depend on for daily life are produced

> by a complex interplay of biological, geological and chemical cycles driven by solar energy and operating across a wide range of spatial and temporal scales. Soil fertility, for instance, is a product both of bacteria, whose fleeting lives may take place in a space smaller than the period at the end of this sentence, as well as of the aeonic, planet-wide cycles of major chemical elements such as carbon and nitrogen. Pest control is created by both natural enemies (e.g., birds; bats; parasitic wasps, ladybugs, spiders, and other predacious arthropods; fungi; viruses) and by climate patterns generated globally. The stratospheric ozone layer that shields Earth's surface from ultraviolet radiation was originally produced primarily by the photosynthetic activities of blue-green algae and by photochemical reactions occurring high in the atmosphere. Ecosystem services operate on such a grand scale and in such intricate and little-explored ways that most could not be replaced by technology.

It is these complex systems that human economic activity is now, for the first time, affecting significantly. Because they provide us with essential services, we need to develop institutions that manage our impacts and ensure the continuation of a natural environment that is supportive of human life. The challenges that this poses arise on many scales, from global to local. Atmospheric changes are the most global, and human activity is now driving three important atmospheric changes—in the carbon and nitrogen cycles and in the ozone layer.

The Global Carbon Cycle

The Earth's atmosphere is principally made up of nitrogen and oxygen with traces of other gases, the most important of which is carbon dioxide. Oxygen is essential for animals: we breathe it and use it to generate energy by oxidizing our food. Humans (along with other animals) breathe in oxygen and breathe out carbon dioxide, the product of burning carbohydrates in our food via the oxygen in our blood. One might expect our use of oxygen would lead to a drop in its content in the air and an increase in carbon dioxide, but this has not occurred because green plants and photosynthetic algae in the seas have the opposite effect. They take in carbon dioxide and emit oxygen, so that there is a natural cycle of oxygen and carbon dioxide.

In fact this process is a small part of a more complex global carbon cycle (see Figure 1.1). The production side involves the production of carbon dioxide by animals and by natural processes, such as the decay of vegetation and weathering of rocks. On the consumption side, carbon dioxide is dissolved in the oceans, absorbed by plants, and stored in the soil as a result of bacterial processes. Human activity is now affecting this cycle in many ways. One is the

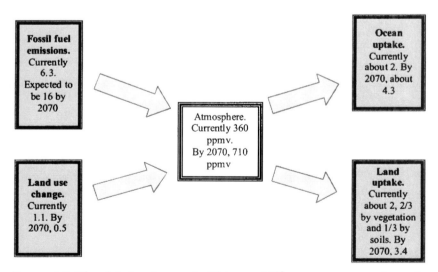

FIGURE 1.1. The global carbon cycle. Units are 10^{15} grams per year unless otherwise stated; ppmv = parts per million by volume. Adapted from Schimel, *Nature,* vol. 393, May 21, 1998, pp. 208–9.

release of massive amounts of carbon dioxide from the burning of fossil fuels; another is changes to the vegetative cover of the planet. Climatic changes may be a by-product of this process, hence current concerns about global warming. The carbon cycle is a good example of the complexity of natural life-support processes, involving oceans, plants, animals, soil, and rocks. It not only provides a gaseous environment in which plants and animals can thrive, but it also affects the Earth's climate and produces temperatures and humidity levels that are comfortable for plants and animals.

We can think of the carbon cycle as a core component of the Earth's HVAC (heating, ventilation, and air-conditioning) system. Until very recently its scale rendered it immune to human activity; that has now changed. The proportion of carbon dioxide in the atmosphere has increased by one-third since the Industrial Revolution, from 280 parts per million to 350, largely because of human activity. It is expected to reach 400 to 500 parts per million in the foreseeable future.

The Nitrogen Cycle

Another basic global chemical cycle is the nitrogen cycle. Plants need nitrogen to grow. There is nitrogen in abundance in the air, but most plants cannot use it in that form. They need nitrogen in chemical form. A small number of plants, such as legumes, can take nitrogen from the air, change its form, and use it for growth. These so-called nitrogen-fixing plants in fact do not directly fix nitrogen themselves; they do it with the assistance of microorganisms that live in colonies around their roots. These plants take in nitrogen, and when they die and are decomposed by the actions of microorganisms, nitrogen is released into the soil and enriches it, providing a better growing medium for other plants that lack the ability to fix nitrogen.

Nitrogen also finds its way into the soil along other pathways, such as the decomposition of dead animals and animal feces. Lightning can also generate fixed nitrogen. Eventually some of the nitrogen in the soil is released back into the atmosphere by microbial action, and some of the plant nitrogen is released into the air by decay. This constitutes the nitrogen cycle.

Human beings have had an even bigger impact on this cycle than on the carbon cycle. Many fertilizers are rich in nitrogen; the quantities of nitrogen added to the soil through fertilizers now exceed the totals fixed through natural processes (Daily, Matson, et al. 1997; Vitousek, Mooney, et al. 1997). We have doubled the scale of the nitrogen cycle. Typically less than half of the total nitrogen added as fertilizer is taken up by plants; nitrogen and its compounds are highly mobile, so the majority runs off into groundwater and ends up in lakes or the sea or seeps through the ground into aquifers. In all of these water bodies there are increasing levels of nitrogen as a result of human modification of the nitrogen cycle.

These modifications have effects on many other aspects of the natural environment. For example, increased nitrogen levels in the ocean lead to changes in marine vegetation and in fish populations. They have also been linked to outbreaks of algae in so-called algal blooms, which have killed millions of fish, damaged fisheries, and rendered beaches unusable for recreation. In tropical countries increased nitrogen levels in seawater are affecting coral reef systems, changing marine vegetation in a manner detrimental to the health of the reefs and the populations living around them. Coral reefs play an important role as spawning grounds for fish and as nurseries for immature fish, so that changes can damage valuable fisheries. Finally, nitrogen released from soil can be converted by bacterial action into oxides of nitrogen that, released into the atmosphere, act as powerful greenhouse gases.

The Ozone Layer

Research is also documenting apparent compromises to the ozone layer, the layer of chemically reactive oxygen high in the atmosphere that serves to screen out some of the ultraviolet radiation hitting the Earth from the sun. Unchecked, this radiation would cause cell damage to living organisms, leading to increased incidence of cancer among animals and lower productivity of plants. Biologists believe that life as we know it might not have evolved without the ozone layer. As is now common knowledge, chemicals used in refrigerators and aerosols are drifting high into the atmosphere and reacting with ozone to neutralize it, removing the protection that it has historically provided.

Impacts on Human Societies

What additional evidence is there that we are stressing the planet's capacity to support human activity, and how convincing is it? Books such as *Extinctions* (Ehrlich and Ehrlich 1981); *Climate Change 1995: The Science of Climate Change* (Houghton, Filho, et al. 1996); *The Work of Nature* (Baskin 1997); *Nature's Services: Societal Dependence on Natural Ecosystems* (Daily 1997); and *Life in the Balance: Humanity and the Biodiversity Crisis* (Eldridge 1998) provide authoritative treatment of these issues. Although there is disagreement regarding the effects, we can summarize the evidence. We've already looked at the impact of human activities on the atmosphere—the carbon cycle, the nitrogen cycle, and the ozone layer. Emissions of carbon dioxide will lead to a doubling of the atmospheric concentration of carbon dioxide within the lifetimes of the younger readers of this book (Houghton, Filho, et al. 1996). There is general agreement that this increase will have a significant impact on the Earth's climate, possibly seriously negative in many places. The numbers cited for possible temperature changes sound small—an increase of 2 to 6 degrees Fahrenheit in global mean temperature. In fact this is not small: it is almost of the same size as the change in temperature between an ice age and the periods that precede and follow it. In the last ice age, a glacier several thousand feet thick covered New York. Another perspective on such a change in climate is provided by the 1997–98 El Niño event, which led to massive weather-related damage. It was associated with an increase in global mean temperature of only about one-half of a degree Fahrenheit, yet in addition to damaging crops and causing widespread weather-induced damage to homes and roads and other infrastructure, it led to massive damage to many critical ecosystems. The dryness caused by the droughts associated with El Niño contributed to huge fires in the Amazon region and in parts of Indonesia, resulting in the loss of hundreds of thousands of acres of tropical forest. As observed earlier, tropical forests help remove carbon from the air; they also play what may be an even more important role in providing a habitat for species found in few other places.

The El Niño events of 1991–92 and 1997–98 also had important impacts in terms of public health. The ranges of various disease-carrying insects and animals depend on climate, and the climatic changes during these years were sufficient to increase the range of the insects carrying malaria, dengue fever, and other dangerous diseases. Weather conditions in these years also contributed to increases in the populations of disease-carrying animals such as mice, leading, for example, to outbreaks of the hantavirus in parts of the United States. It seems that even small climatic changes, of the magnitude well within those forecast, can potentially lead to significant public health concerns (McMichael 1993; Epstein 1998; Epstein 1999).

In addition to the global impacts our activity has on atmospheric systems, we are compromising important ecosystem services on more local scales. For example, our freshwater resources provide a link between the local and global systems. They are dependent on the hydrological cycle and so are affected by global climate change, but they are also influenced by local phenomena such as land use. Freshwater resources are endangered by human activity: humans now consume more than 50 percent of all the renewable accessible freshwater falling on land (Postel, Daily, et al. 1996). Freshwater is of course a critical resource for human societies, and while it can in principle be replaced by distilled seawater, the costs of producing and transporting distilled seawater are high enough to force big changes in our lifestyles. Desalinated water currently costs about six times the average cost of urban water supplies, at least ten times the average cost of water to farmers (Postel and Carpenter 1997). Even areas where energy is plentiful and water transportation easy place a high premium on control of freshwater supplies.

The fate of fisheries also illustrates the links between the global and the local. Climate change and changes in the nitrogen cycle are affecting the productivity of fisheries, and together with mismanagement of local fisheries they are exhausting the capacities of the oceans to provide fish to meet our food needs. The productivity of many major fisheries has plummeted in recent years, and fisheries biologists believe that for some key species the populations will never recover (Botsford, Castillo, et al. 1997).

There are many other ways in which we are affecting the biology of the Earth at the regional level. For example, we are introducing over 5,000 exotic species every year to new biogeographic realms (Drake

1989) and are dramatically altering patterns of land cover. One result of these changes is an extinction spasm as great as any in geologic history (Ehrlich and Ehrlich 1981; Ehrlich 1988). The Earth is now losing species at a rate unparalleled since the extinction of the nonavian dinosaurs. Possibly as many as 27,000 species are lost to extinction every year (Wilson 1938; Eldridge 1998; Hughes, Daily, et al. 1997).

Another worrying localized phenomenon is the loss of soil and the reduction of soil fertility. Vast quantities of productive soil are being lost every year to erosion by wind and rain, quantities equivalent to tens of thousands of acres of productive land. Elsewhere soil fertility is being reduced by excessive use. Scientists have estimated that up to 17 percent of the Earth's arable land has been degraded by soil loss or by overuse that has reduced its fertility. Fertility reduction can be reversed by leaving the soil fallow, but for severely depleted soil this may take decades or even centuries (Daily, Matson, et al. 1997; Hughes, Daily, et al. 1997).

Biodiversity

A different perspective on the role of the natural environment comes from a discussion of biodiversity. Biodiversity, or biological diversity, refers to the diversity of plant, animal, insect, and microorganism species. The diversity of life on Earth is a product of the carbon and nitrogen cycles and other local and global ecosystems. Biodiversity exists at many different levels: at the level of an ecosystem, a community, a population. Biodiversity is the variation between and within species at and between all of these levels. Scientists are beginning to believe that biodiversity is of considerable importance in many ways. Let's look at some of these now; there will be many more examples in later chapters.

A dramatic example of the direct importance of diversity to humans comes from the recent history of rice production. The prosperity and comfort of literally billions of people depend on rice harvests. In the 1970s, the grassy stunt virus, a new virus carried by the brown plant hopper, threatened the Asian rice crop. The virus appeared capable of destroying a large fraction of the crop; in some years it destroyed as much as one-quarter. Developing a form of rice resistant to this virus became of critical importance.

Rice breeders succeeded in this task with the help of the International Rice Research Institute (IRRI) in the Philippines. The IRRI conducts research on rice production and holds a large bank of seeds—about 80,000 different varieties of rice and the near-relatives of rice. In this case the IRRI located a single strain of wild rice that was not used commercially and was resistant to the grassy stunt virus. The gene conveying resistance was transferred to commercial rice varieties, yielding commercial rice resistant to the threatening virus.

This would not have been possible without the genes from a strain of rice that was apparently of no commercial value; without this variety, the world's rice crop, one of its most important food crops, would have been seriously damaged by the new virus. The strain of wild rice that was resistant to the virus was found in only one location, a valley that was flooded by a hydroelectric dam shortly after the IRRI found the critical rice variety and took it into its collection. The same story was repeated later in the 1970s, and similar stories have occurred with other food crops, in particular corn in the United States (Myers 1997).

We have every reason to expect that events like these will recur regularly: planting large areas with genetically identical plants greatly increases the chances that once a disease starts, it will spread with dangerous speed through the entire area and crop. *The Benefits of Biodiversity,* a 1999 report by the Council for Agricultural Science and Technology, emphasized this point:

> Because of the increasingly high densities and large areas over which they are now grown, both livestock and crop plants are continually acquiring new diseases and pests, and existing diseases and pests are continually evolving new strains that overcome the defenses of particular breeds or strains. This is exaggerated by the accidental transport of diseases around the world. These diseases and pests destabilize agricultural systems. . . . Indeed, catastrophic attacks of disease, invasions of insects, and climatic extremes have caused wholesale crop destruction and ensuing famines whenever crops had insufficient diversity to provide at least some plants with the ability to withstand the assaults. . . . The continual accrual of new

diseases can be countered only if breeders can find sufficient genetic diversity within a crop or its relatives. Even
the full complement of natural genetic variation, though,
may not be sufficient to stop some diseases. . . . A lethal
disease of corn, or wheat or rice, were it to appear, would
devastate agriculture and human society. The only insurance that society has against such a catastrophe is biodiversity. Genetic diversity within a crop plant or animal
species and its relatives might allow resistant strains to be
discovered and used. Similarly, a diversity of potential
food plants might allow another species to become an
effective substitute for a major crop species that was lost
to disease.

To summarize, biological diversity has proven to be a valuable
resource: the availability of genetic material different from that currently used provides a buffer against threats to essential food crops,
and diversity of populations acts as a barrier to the rapid transmis-
sion of diseases. But biodiversity in all its aspects is threatened by
current developments (Hughes, Daily, et al. 1997). The availability
of diverse genetic material has also proven central to bringing about
more routine improvements in crop productivity and to the green
revolution that has allowed food production in developing countries
to keep up with their population growth. Many productivity
increases have been attained by incorporating into existing commercial varieties of plants genetic material from other varieties or
species. In these examples, biodiversity has acted in two ways: it has
played the role of an insurance policy, allowing us to recover from
potentially dangerous threats; and it has provided us with knowledge
about alternative genetic structures and their properties. This is technical scientific knowledge that would have been difficult, if not
impossible, to develop otherwise. Both of these roles may be com-
promised by the significant reduction now occurring in the numbers
of extant species.

Destroying Our Ecological Foundation: A Cautionary Example

The importance of the ecological infrastructure underpinning our
way of life can be seen from historical examples of societies that have
collapsed probably as a result of overstressing their ecosystems. One

widely cited example, the civilization of Easter Island, is discussed here, though similar points are exemplified by the Maoris in New Zealand and by parts of the Maya civilization.

Easter Island (also called Rapa Nui) is a small Pacific island over 2,000 miles from the coast of Chile, with a population of about 2,100. The civilization of Easter Island was from its first contact with Europeans to recent time a great enigma. Only massive stone heads, *moai,* looking out to sea remained to tell the story of the island's early inhabitants. The largest of these weighed 80 tons; one, weighing over 270 tons, rested in the quarry where it was carved. Their presence indicates that a powerful society once made this its home.

The Polynesian society in place at the time of European discovery was clearly poorer and less technically skilled than those that had preceded it. It seemed incapable of creating such monumental architecture and too poor to support a large artisan class devoted to carving statues; indeed, there was no such group in the eighteenth century. Equally puzzling is that the statues were moved a substantial distance from the island's lone quarry to their final destinations. The population, estimated at about 3,000 in 1722, seemed too small to move the larger statues, at least without tools such as levers, rollers, rope, or wooden sleds. Furthermore, the island in 1722 had no trees suitable for making such tools. Local residents had no knowledge of how to move the statues and believed that they had walked to the platforms under the influence of a spiritual power.

The history of Easter Island appears to involve prosperity and sophistication, followed by collapse. Over time there have been many speculations about the nature and origins of this civilization and about its mysterious demise. The reigning theory is that its population grew so large that all land and sea bird populations were hunted to extinction, all inshore fisheries were exhausted, and the palm forests that once covered the islands were destroyed for agriculture, leading to soil erosion. Consequently the population was unable to support itself and collapsed in a spasm of civil war and possibly cannibalism.

It is now believed that Easter Island was first settled by a small group of Polynesians about A.D. 400. The pollen record shows that the island supported a great palm forest at this time. Initially the first settlers cut down trees to make canoes, which they used to catch fish. The wood from these was also used to make tools and for firewood. The forests on the island supported a large population of nesting birds that were a part of the islanders' diet. The population appears to have grown rapidly, and the inhabitants were wealthy in the sense that after meeting their subsistence requirements, they would have had ample time to devote to other activities, including, as time went on, carving and moving their great stone statues.

After five centuries, i.e., by A.D. 900, the record shows a reduction in pollen. Most of the statues were carved shortly after this, between about A.D. 1100 and 1500. By A.D. 1400 the palm forests had vanished completely. As a result the population, which may have reached a peak of about 10,000 in 1400, began to decline.

The carving of statues ceased around this time, and more or less simultaneously a new tool resembling a spearhead or dagger appears in the archaeological record. At the same time, islanders began to live in caves and fortified homes, and there is evidence of cannibalism. All of this suggests a period of violent disorder and conflict, in sharp contrast with the apparent organization and stability of the earlier eras. This period of disorder led to the state of Easter Island's society recorded by the first Europeans to visit.

The short explanation of the collapse is that the islanders had degraded their environment to the point where it could no longer support the resident population. While the evidence certainly supports this interpretation, it is not clear why this happened on Easter Island and not on all other islands settled by the Polynesians. Easter Island was not unique in experiencing this type of collapse, but most of the other islands that went through this experience were smaller and had less developed and less distinctive cultures.

A recent analysis summarized a possible explanation of the unique fate of Easter Island in the following terms (Diamond 1995; Brander and Taylor 1998) (the quote is from Brander and Taylor):

> It (Easter Island) was an outlier in one very important respect. The palm tree that grew on Easter Island (*Jubea chilensis*) happened to be a very slow-growing palm. . . . This palm tree grows nowhere else in Polynesia, and it is

perhaps the only palm that can live in Easter Island's relatively cool climate. An authoritative text reports that "Cultivation presents few problems in a suitable temperate climate, but growth of these massive palms is slow and it is generally later generations who benefit from the plantings." Under ideal conditions this palm requires about 40 to 60 years before it reaches the fruit-growing stage, and it can take longer.

In contrast, the two most common large palms in Polynesia are the Cocos and the Pritchardia. Neither of these palms can grow on Easter Island, and both are fast-growing trees that reach fruit-growing age in approximately seven to ten years.

The authors conclude, on the basis of computer modeling of the interactions between the human population and the palm forest that provided its natural base, that the slow-growing palm could have supported a steady and prosperous population only through careful management of the demands placed on it. A combination of population control and sustainable use of the forests might have kept the early civilization alive. Rapid population growth and uncontrolled use led to the destruction of the palm forests and the consequent loss of methods of construction, heating, cooking, and fishing. It also led to the loss of bird and animal populations, dooming the civilization. In the end the people of Easter Island were left with little food, no building material, and no way of making seafaring craft by which they could escape from their self-imposed misery.

The conclusion from this and other cases is that ecological stresses can contribute to social collapse. But there is another, more positive, side to this coin: propitious ecological conditions support human progress. This point is beautifully argued by Jared Diamond in *Guns, Germs, and Steel* (1997), which suggests close links between the ability of ecosystems in some parts of the world to provide key services to human societies and the rapid material progress of those societies. The services at issue include food production, power (from domesticated draft animals), provision of precursors to textile fabrics, and, of course, productive and stable climates. Diamond's argument could be paraphrased by saying that the Middle East was the cradle of civilization because of an unusually favorable conjunction of ecosystem services, and that several of the initially successful civilizations in this area met their ends by undermining the very systems that brought them into being—for example, by salination of the valleys of the Tigris and Euphrates.

Clearly these examples are of societies far different from ours, less technologically sophisticated and so more obviously dependent on their natural infrastructures. Yet climate stability, food production, and disease control (a key issue in Diamond's analysis) are still essential to our own societies, and our potential impacts on the systems that affect these and other services are therefore a matter of concern.

Biosphere 2

The previous examples describe the fate that befalls human societies that destroy their ecological foundations. The next example, far more recent, provides a rather different illustration of the complexity of the natural mechanisms that provide essential services to us. It shows us that as sophisticated and knowledgeable as we are, we cannot use our technologies to replace the services that natural ecosystems provide.

Biosphere 2 is an ecosystem sealed in glass and covering 3.15 acres in Oracle, Arizona. It was constructed at great expense—roughly $200 million in 1991 dollars—to investigate the possibility that a completely self-contained system could support eight people for two years. There would be no exchange with the outside world except for energy supplied to run appliances. The intent was that the eight "biospherians" would grow all their own food and that the system would operate with a fixed volume of air and water, which would be recycled and reused as they are in the original Biosphere 1, the Earth.

After the start of this experiment in 1991, the managers experienced numerous completely unexpected problems. One and a half years after the closure of Biosphere 2, the oxygen content of the atmosphere had fallen from 21 percent to 14 percent, a level normally found at 17,500 feet and barely sufficient to keep the biospherians functioning. Levels of carbon dioxide and nitrous oxide skyrocketed. Additionally, all of the pollinators had become extinct

(Cohen and Tilman 1996). The drop in oxygen levels and increase in carbon dioxide levels means that Biosphere's systems were incapable of replicating the activities of the carbon cycle, the most essential natural cycle for human life. The extinction of all pollinators implies that agricultural production would rapidly have declined. In summary, in spite of great expense and the use of the most sophisticated technologies, the designers of Biosphere 2 were unable to build in the capacity to replicate some of the most basic and essential services that natural ecosystems provide to human societies. Not only are the services of these systems essential, but it also appears that most of them cannot be replaced by technological substitutes.

Summary

Natural systems contribute to human welfare. Acting at a variety of scales from truly global to very local, they provide the infrastructure upon which we build our homes and our societies. We are affecting these in a variety of ways, many unprecedented. Humans are now, perhaps inadvertently, one of the main drivers of the evolution of the planet. This extraordinary power brings with it extraordinary dangers, specifically, the danger that before we understand fully what is happening we shall inflict irreversible damage on natural systems for which we have no replacements. There are certainly historical precedents for this.

The remaining chapters discuss possible economic institutions for managing our impact on the planet and the essential infrastructure it provides for us. Currently we are economically blind to these impacts: our economic institutions disregard them. Measures of economic welfare or of economic performance neglect damage to planetary infrastructures. Economic policies have traditionally been designed and evaluated without reference to impacts on planetary systems. These things need not be so: there are changes in our economic institutions that could certainly improve on the present situation, though it is not yet clear whether they would be fully adequate for the tasks. Indeed, the Kyoto Protocol proposes economic institutions that could have far-reaching and positive effects on carbon emissions and also on the destruction of tropical forests. These are markets for the right to emit greenhouse gases, and we will be looking at them in detail later in this book. They are a partial answer to the general question, How should economic institutions be adapted to cope well with the scale of human impacts on the biosphere? Can we rely on markets, or do we need different economic mechanisms? How should we redefine our measures of economic performance to reflect impacts on planetary systems? All of these are the agenda of this book. We begin that agenda in Chapter 2 with a few basic economic principles.

Chapter 2

Basic Economics

Market economic systems operate by giving people and businesses opportunities to increase their incomes by providing goods and services that others need and want. These opportunities to earn income are the incentive that drives economic activity in market economies and that drives people to provide goods and services.

The relative profitabilities of different activities determine how attractive they are: more profitable opportunities are generally chosen over less profitable ones. Prices play a crucial role in determining profitability and are therefore important in determining the most attractive opportunities. *Profit* is the difference between revenues from sales of goods and services and the costs of making or providing those goods and services. *Revenue* is the quantities sold multiplied by their prices; similarly, cost is the quantities of inputs used multiplied by their prices. So prices play a big role in creating incentive. High prices for outputs make a venture attractive, as do low prices for inputs. The opposite is also true: low prices of outputs or high prices of inputs make a venture unattractive.

PROFIT = REVENUE – COST
= PRICE OF OUTPUT × QUANTITY OF OUTPUT
– PRICE OF INPUT × QUANTITY OF INPUT

If an economic system is working well, the incentives driving individuals and businesses should lead them in directions that are desirable from a social perspective. Market incentives should, in other words, lead people to provide such goods and services and to provide them by such processes as are appropriate socially.

This statement raises an obvious question: What does it mean to be "appropriate" from a social perspective? Economists have given this concept the technical name *Pareto efficiency,* after the Italian economist Vilfredo Pareto, who first suggested the concept, and a very specific meaning:

> An economy is Pareto efficient if it is operating in such a way that no one can be made better off without someone else being made worse off.

In an intuitive sense, an economy is Pareto efficient if it operates with no slack—that is, it operates so that there is no way of making everyone better off, or at least some people better off and none worse off, so that all "win-win" opportunities are exploited. So to rephrase the earlier statement, if an economy is operating well, the incentives it gives to people and businesses should lead them to a pattern of production and consumption that is Pareto efficient—i.e., to one where there is no slack, where all opportunities for mutual gain are fully realized.

One of the most fundamental insights into the operation of a competitive market economy is that under certain conditions it will do exactly this: it will align individual and social interests and provide incentives that lead to a Pareto-efficient outcome. In the famous words of Adam Smith (1977) in *An Inquiry into the Nature and Causes of the Wealth of Nations* (first published in 1776),

> Every individual . . . neither intends to promote the public interest, nor knows how much he is promoting it. He intends only his own security, his own gain. And he is in this led by an invisible hand to promote an end which was no part of his intention. By pursuing his own interest he frequently promotes that of society more effectively than when he really intends to promote it.

This is an apt metaphor: market forces are an invisible hand steering us to act in the interests of society as a whole when in fact we seek only to promote our own. In the 1950s some important propositions from economic theory formalized this insight and made it more precise. These propositions state that under the conditions enumerated below, a competitive market economy is Pareto efficient—i.e., it operates so as to leave unexploited no possibilities for mutual gain.

This is a remarkable result and provides the basis for economists' belief in the efficacy of market systems and the desirability of market-based approaches to economic organization. It is remarkable for several reasons. A market economy is decentralized: there is no one in control and no one making decisions about what is produced, how it is produced, or what prices should be charged. Consumers, millions of them, decide individually and largely independently what and how much to consume. Producers, thousands if not millions of them, decide simultaneously what and how much to produce. Then, in spite of the lack of formal or explicit coordination, what producers decided to produce matches what consumers decided to consume, both in type and in amount. Furthermore, this happens in an overall pattern that is Pareto efficient. It is little short of miraculous that such a complex and uncoordinated system should lead to coherent and efficient outcomes rather than to total chaos. We take this for granted: we have lived with it all our lives and would be amazed if it did not happen.

People from different backgrounds see matters very differently. There are fascinating stories of Soviet economic planners visiting market economies in the heyday of their economic system, in which everything was planned centrally, and coming away impressed by how smoothly Western economies operated. On one occasion, one of the visiting economists took his host aside and said to him: "We are very impressed. But how do you hide your planners so well?" He could not conceive that a complex economic system could operate so effectively without central guidance.

Of course, the key to understanding this is Adam Smith's "invisible hand." There is no explicit coordination, but there is coordination nonetheless, through prices. If demand for a good exceeds its supply, then its price rises, strengthening incentives to produce it. Conversely, should supply of a good exceed the demand for it, then its price will fall, leading to less incentive for its production. If an input to production is scarce, then its price will rise, directing producers both to economize on its use and also to develop substitutes. For example, when the price of oil was high in the late 1970s and early 1980s, immense ingenuity went into finding more and into economizing its use. Oil use per unit of output fell 40 percent in the United States from 1974 to 1984. At the same time, the world's reserves of oil increased enormously (Heal and Chichilnisky 1991).

This is the invisible hand at work. Of course, it is not literally a hand, and in reality it is visible: it is a list of prices and a set of forces determining them. And it is our society's primary mechanism for making economic decisions. In the realm of resource economics, we have to ask whether it can work for planetary systems and ecosystems as well as it has worked for food, fuel, communications, and many other requirements of daily life.

Figure 2.1 summarizes what has been said so far about the market and the invisible hand. The market controls how the resources available to a society and the technological skills and knowledge at its command are combined to determine what is produced, how it is produced, who consumes it, and the prices at which it sells. These in turn affect people's well-being. In all of this the market is guided by people's preferences, by what they want to consume.

Clearly we can all think of situations where this invisible hand seems to be doing a good job and others where it is less satisfactory. For the United States in the last few decades it seems to have done a remarkably good job with respect to the high-technology sector. It has provided incentives to innovate that have led to important new products, relatively clean products, and new employment and widespread prosperity in major regions of the country. Something similar could be said of the financial sector, which has likewise produced new products and prosperity. These situations contrast sharply with many others—for example, the fishing industry. Commercial fishing has destroyed the basis of its own prosperity through overfishing to the point where many species that were once commercially important are now close to extinction. In the process it has inflicted great

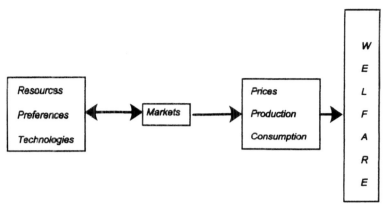

FIGURE 2.1. Using technologies and guided by preferences, the market transforms resources into goods and services that meet human needs.

damage on natural marine ecosystems. In a different sphere, the same Internet and electronic systems that have brought prosperity to many have also facilitated a boom in pornography: this is apparently very profitable. But all these very diverse activities are responses to market-generated incentives. What distinguishes the good cases from the bad?

Answering this question requires some more economics background. It also requires that we return to a topic mentioned but not addressed earlier, that "under the conditions enumerated below, a competitive market economy is Pareto efficient." The good and bad outcomes of the market are distinguished by the nature of the goods being traded.

There are two main conditions that the goods traded must satisfy if the invisible hand is to work well and the market outcome is to be efficient:

> The first is that all goods and services traded should be private rather than public goods. The second is that there are no differences between the private and social costs of producing the goods or services.

Also, we need to be sure that the economy is, as stated in the proposition, a competitive economy, which means that there should be significant competition among producers offering the main goods and services. This is precisely the concern of bodies such as the Department of Justice and the Federal Trade Commission in the

United States and their equivalents in other countries: it is in pursuit of the goal of a competitive environment that the Department of Justice is currently battling with Microsoft, having previously done so with Standard Oil, AT&T, and IBM, among others.

Private and Social Costs and Benefits

What does it mean that there should be no differences between private and social costs and that all goods and services should be private rather than public? Let's first look at the issue of private and social costs.

The private costs of an activity are those incurred by the person or business carrying it out. The social costs are the total costs incurred by society as a result of the activity. They include the private costs but may also include other items as well. What is required by the equality of private and social costs and benefits is that the costs that a producer incurs in using a good should include all the costs that its use of the good imposes on society, and that there should be no costs to society that are not also costs to the producer.

Differences between private and social costs are known as "external effects"; the reason for this terminology will be clear later. Consider as an illustration of private and social costs the use of an automobile for transportation: the driver incurs costs from using the car—wear and tear on the car, the need to have it serviced, and so forth. He or she also incurs fuel and time costs. These are the private costs: they lead to bills the user must pay. In this case, the payments the driver makes clearly do not match, and are not equivalent to, the costs imposed on society by the use of the car. Society has to repair wear and tear on the roads and in addition has to cope with the pollution and congestion generated by vehicle use. So in this case the social costs of the activity exceed the private costs. They exceed the private costs by the amount of costs that the use of the vehicle imposes on others—congestion, pollution, wear and tear on roads—for which the user does not have to compensate those who bear them.[1]

---

1. There are other sources of private-social cost differences. Ill-considered government policies can easily drive a wedge between the two. Tariffs, nontariff barriers, and certain taxes are some of the most common examples.

What about commercial fishing? Does it meet the condition of no private-social cost differences? It does not, although in this case the difference is subtler than in the case of automobile use. The point in this case is that there is a fixed stock of fish in a fishery at any point of time, and the more fish caught by one boat, the fewer will be left for others. If I catch more, you will probably catch less. Not only do you catch less; all other boats will catch less. So the social costs of my activities include the cost of you and others catching less. This is not a private cost to me; it is, however, a cost to you. If you have difficulty understanding this, consider the extreme case in which I get to the fishing ground first and catch all available fish. Obviously much of my success is at your expense. So again there is a difference between private and social costs.

Why does it matter that private and social costs coincide? The invisible hand works efficiently when it aligns private pursuit of gain with the public good. This is the message in the quote from Adam Smith. Private and social costs coincide when the costs that a decision-maker takes into account are all the costs that matter to society. In this case, by choosing what to him is the least expensive way of doing something, he also chooses the way that is least expensive from the social perspective. Similarly, by seeking the most profitable opportunities, he seeks not only to maximize the added value according to his own calculations but also according to society's calculus.

When private and social costs coincide, we have this desirable alignment of interests. What is least expensive for you or me is also least expensive for society as a whole. What is best for you or me is also best for society as a whole. In situations like this it is indeed the case, as Alfred P. Sloan once said, that what is good for General Motors is good for America.

When private and social costs differ, things go wrong. Suppose I have a choice between transportation methods A and B and that A is less expensive for me but has a large difference between private and social costs. The cost to me is, say, $10, and the social cost is $15. For B, the cost to me, which is $12, is also the total social cost. Then I will naturally choose method A, with a cost to me of $10, in preference to method B, with its cost to me of $12. From a social perspective I am making the wrong choice: I am choosing the option that imposes

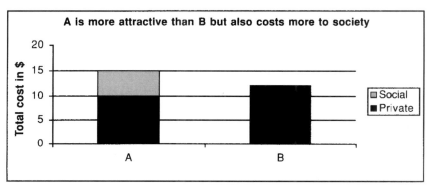

FIGURE 2.2. Choice *A* has lower private costs ($10) but higher social costs ($15) than *B* and so will be chosen although it imposes a greater burden on society.

greater costs on society. I am choosing *A* with social cost $15 over *B* with social cost $12, imposing the unnecessary cost of $3 on society. So price, the invisible hand, only aligns private and public interests if private and social costs are equal. Otherwise the private and public interests may diverge. Figure 2.2 illustrates this concept.

So far the discussion has focused on differences between the private and social costs of an activity. There may also be differences between the private and social *benefits* of doing something. Planting a forest may bring some gains to the landowner, in terms of income from timber sales. But it may bring much bigger gains to society as a whole, because the forest sequesters carbon and provides an environment for animal life. Driving a more fuel-efficient car may bring financial gains to the driver. Society may gain by more than the fuel savings because of the reduction in greenhouse gas emissions. Just as we will tend to do too much of the activities whose social costs exceed the private costs, so will we also do too little of those for which social benefits exceed private benefits.

| PRIVATE COST < SOCIAL COST | TOO MUCH |
| PRIVATE BENEFIT < SOCIAL BENEFIT | TOO LITTLE |

Figure 2.3 summarizes what we have learned about differences in private and social costs. It reproduces Figure 2.1, with two additions. It shows that natural ecosystems affect society's welfare and that the

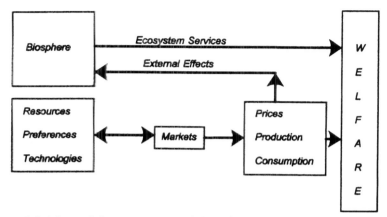

FIGURE 2.3. Many of the services provided by the natural environment do not go through the market, and some market activities affect the environment.

operation of the market affects natural ecosystems in ways external to the market. This, incidentally, is the genesis of the term "external effect": it is an effect external to the market and therefore not mediated by or controlled by the market.

Public Goods

Now to the second condition, that all goods and services traded must be private rather than public. What is the difference between public and private goods? Most goods are private goods. They are goods for which consumption is "rival" and "excludable." Consumption is "rival" when my consumption of the good competes with or rivals yours: if I consume it, then you cannot. This is obviously true for goods like food, wine, housing, gasoline, and seats at the opera. If I consume a unit of one of these, then you cannot consume that same unit. You and I compete for the consumption of a given unit. Of course, there may be other units, so that this competition does not prevent both of us from getting what we want.

Not all goods are like this. If I consume a TV broadcast, you are not prevented from doing so as well. My benefiting from enhanced law and order does not exclude you from doing so too. These are goods that benefit all members of a community.

Excludability means something different. It means that the seller can ensure that only those who have paid for a good consume it. In case this sounds obvious, think about computer software. You can buy it, install it on your machine, and then let a friend install from the same disks on his machine. Of course this is illegal, but in spite of that it surely happens. So a software maker cannot exclude those who do not pay from using the product. The same is true for book publishers: they cannot be sure that you do not copy their products and distribute them free of charge, so they cannot exclude nonpayers from reading. Again, this would be illegal, but it is certainly possible. This problem does not arise with food, wine, opera seats, furniture, cars, airline seats, and, indeed, most goods.

So public goods are goods that are nonrival and nonexcludable, goods for which my consumption does not compete with yours and whose providers cannot exclude from their use those who have not paid for them.

Defense is a classic example of a public good. If the defense system of our country is improved for me, then it is improved for you. Your enjoyment of the benefits of the improvement does not detract from mine. There is no rivalry in our consumption of defense. At the same time, defense is not excludable. The Department of Defense cannot decide to defend the country for some of its citizens and not others. It defends all of us or none of us. In this sense defense is a very socialist activity—somewhat ironic, given its usual position in political debate.

Air quality is also a public good: if it is conserved for one, it is conserved for all. The benefits I obtain from clean air do not detract from yours. In fact, many environmental goods are public goods. There are also intermediate goods that have some of the characteristics of both private and public goods, such as scrambled TV broadcasts. Those who do not subscribe to unscramblers cannot receive them, so providers can exclude them. However, there is still no rivalry in consumption.

Why does it matter if a good is public or private? Markets do not work very well for public goods, at least not conventional markets. There are innovations in this area happening right now, some embodied in the Kyoto Protocol and in the 1990 Clean Air Act of the United States. Both of these are attempts to use markets to control the provision of a public good. The problem with public goods is that the market provides inadequate incentives for their provision. The main reason is their nonexcludability—the fact that the seller cannot prevent nonpayers from benefiting from them. If a good is really public, I have little incentive to buy it for myself. I may as well wait for you or someone else to buy it, let them pay, and then enjoy the benefits of their purchase. If the good is really nonexcludable, then this is always possible.

This is what economists call the "free-rider problem": everyone gets a free ride in obtaining a public good provided and financed by someone else. We can restate the problem in the terms used earlier: The social benefits of consuming a public good exceed the private. Why? Because others benefit from my consumption of the good. Examples abound: for instance, if I clean the air in order to consume cleaner air, those near me gain as much as I do.

In the commercial field, these problems are manifested with software and with knowledge. Returning to the earlier example, software can easily be used by people who did not pay for it. Because of this, manufacturers do not receive revenues from all users of their products. The revenues they receive and the profits they make consequently understate the social value of their products. The incentive they have to make their products is less than it should be for overall efficient operation of the economy—hence the interest they have in preventing unauthorized use of their products and the interest the government has in helping them in this.

The same is true, but to an even greater degree, for knowledge. Knowledge is the quintessential public good. I can share my knowledge with you without in any way detracting from my own possession of it. Consequently the producer of the knowledge cannot exclude the possibility that those who did not pay for it will nevertheless benefit from it. So there may be a systematic tendency to underinvest in the provision of knowledge. As knowledge is a key factor in the growth of modern industrial economies, this is potentially a very serious matter.

Many policy measures are directed at this issue, most of them in the area of intellectual property rights. Intellectual property rights legislation is intended to make it easier for producers of knowledge to exclude from using it those who have not paid for it. This is the point of patents, trademarks, and other devices for strengthening intellectual property rights. The role of patents in this context should be clear: they give the producer of knowledge a right to exclude others from using it. Typically they would not be able to do this without such legal support because knowledge is a public good. Its use cannot be limited to those who have paid for its development.

Rather than excluding from its use those who do not fund it and limiting its benefits as a public good, knowledge could alternatively be funded by the public sector and made available to all. This is the approach taken in the United States with basic research and development funded by national agencies such as the National Science Foundation, the National Oceanic and Atmospheric Administration, and the National Institutes of Health. Basic research clearly leads to results that benefit the community as a whole, with implications too broad for any single entity to appropriate.

What is the connection between private and social costs, public goods, and how our economic system can manage the use of the global systems that provide infrastructure for human societies? The key points are that many of the interactions that we have with natural ecosystems are characterized by differences between private and social costs, and that several of the services provided by natural ecosystems are public goods. There are therefore reasons to believe that in these cases unaided markets will not lead to efficient outcomes.

Commercial fishing was cited earlier as one example of private-social cost differences. Burning fossil fuels is another example of such differences: the private costs of using fossil fuels are the costs of the fuel itself and any costs associated with using the combustion equipment. The social costs include these but also the costs imposed on society by increases in the amount of carbon dioxide in the atmosphere and consequent changes in the carbon cycle. Likewise with the use of nitrogen fertilizers: the social cost exceeds the private cost by an amount that reflects the costs of nitrogen running off agricultural land into rivers, aquifers, and the sea and of changing the global nitrogen cycle. The social costs of using chlorofluorocarbons (CFCs) in air conditioners and refrigerators exceed the private costs by the costs imposed on society by a depletion of the ozone layer and the consequent reduction in its ability to shield against ultraviolet radiation. Cutting down forests also has social costs that exceed the private costs; the difference here lies in the loss to society of the carbon sequestration services of the forest and also the loss of its support of biodiversity. Commercial fishing, deforestation, and the use of fossil fuels, nitrogen, and CFCs are all characterized by differences between private and social costs. So in all these cases we cannot expect the unaided market to reach an efficient outcome. In these and in similar cases, of which there are many, the market will lead to more use than is consistent with economic efficiency, because the costs that individuals and businesses face are less than those faced by society. The incentives to use fossil fuels, CFCs, and nitrogen fertilizers and to engage in deforestation are all stronger than they should be for economic efficiency.

Now to public goods. Air quality is a public good. My enjoyment of this clearly does not compete with yours. And if I invest in preserving the present system—for example, by using solar heating and driving a fuel-efficient car—and you do not, then I cannot exclude you from benefiting from my actions. Similarly, if one neighborhood or region cuts back emissions of pollutants and another does not, the former cannot prevent the latter from sharing in the benefits. So air quality meets the two criteria for being a public good.

So too does the ozone layer. It is in many ways like a defense system: if it protects one from ultraviolet radiation, then it protects all. There is no competition in consumption, and if we invest in protecting its effectiveness, we cannot exclude from its benefits those who have not contributed. So we have another set of reasons that markets may not lead to efficient use of important global life-support systems: these are public goods, and the incentive to maintain them and to invest in their conservation may be too low for an efficient outcome. Likewise, the knowledge provided by genetic diversity is a public good.

Taxes and Quotas

Where does this discussion leave us in practical terms? What can we do about these issues? The remainder of this chapter will address these issues in the case of private-social cost differences. Public goods pose more complex problems than private goods, problems that may require nonmarket institutions for their resolution. Chapter 8 deals with these.

Recall that external effects are defined as differences between the private and social costs of an action. Conventionally economists have thought in terms of two principal approaches to the control and correction of external effects. These are control and correction via taxes and subsidies, in a tradition stemming from the work of Pigou (1932), and control and correction via the introduction of property rights, as suggested by Coase (1960).

A. C. Pigou, an economics professor at Cambridge from 1908 to 1943, was the first to analyze the inefficiencies that stem from differences between the private and the social costs of an activity. In his view, these differences between private and social costs were to be corrected by taxes or subsidies: the point of these was to alter the private cost of the activity until it equals the social cost. After correction of these differences, one has the relationship

PRIVATE COST + TAX (OR − SUBSIDY) = SOCIAL COST

The total cost to the person carrying out the activity is now the private cost plus the tax (or minus the subsidy), which is equal to the social cost.

In the case of CO_2 emission, there is the private cost of the fuel burned; the social costs include, in addition to the fuel costs, an increased likelihood of harmful climate change. A corrective tax added to the private cost will bring the private cost into line with the social cost. This is the motivation for taxes such as carbon taxes.

Coase, in contrast, focused on the fact that goods and services can be bought and sold only if they are owned—i.e., if they are someone's property. In other words, goods and services can be brought within the orbit of trading and the market mechanism if they can be owned. Ownership of a good or service means that people can have property rights in it. So Coase saw externalities as arising from the fact that some goods and services are not owned—i.e., from an absence of property rights. Certain economically important goods and services cannot be bought or sold, and therefore neither the market nor the legal system can regulate their provision. These goods and services are external to the market—hence their name "external effects"—and so the market cannot ensure their provision at an efficient level. The natural policy prescription from this perspective is to introduce property rights for the goods and services that do not have them, so that these goods and services can be traded and their provision regulated by the market and by the legal system.

Let's apply this idea to the example of air quality and the use of carbon-based fuels. We can say that the services of the atmosphere are being used as a depository for the products of CO_2 combustion. However, legally there are no property rights in the atmosphere; there is thus no opportunity for people to register a demand for air quality to be left unaltered. So there is no market for air quality, and the market cannot weigh the demand for air quality against the demand to use the air as a dumping ground. There are, in contrast, property rights over land, so that it cannot be used as a depository for waste without permission from the owner, which normally requires payment. The amount of the payment will depend on the value that the landowner places on the cleanliness of his land. According to Coase's view, we need to establish property rights in the atmosphere so that anyone wishing to use it to dump waste must first buy the right to do so from the owner.

Coase did not in fact think in terms of the establishment of property rights leading to the use of a market to control externalities. His insight was that with property rights established there was a framework for bargaining between those affected by the externality and those causing it, and that this bargaining would lead to an efficient outcome. He developed the example of a factory emitting smoke that dirties the washing of a nearby community. Initially there are no property rights on either side, so that the factory is legally free to pollute. Then property rights are introduced. There are two possibilities for this introduction: one is that the factory has the right to use the air however it wishes, and the other is that the community has the right to clean air. In the former case, the factory clearly has a legal right to continue as before, and if the community wishes to stop the pollution they must make it in the interest of the factory to stop. In general this will mean paying the factory to stop; the payment will have to be sufficient to meet the costs of installing antipollution devices. If the community does not feel that the value of stopping the pollution is as high as the cost of antipollution devices, then the pollution will continue. This is as it should be: reducing pollution has costs and benefits and should only be carried out if the latter exceed the former.

Consider now the case in which the community has a right to clean air. Then pollution by the factory will violate the rights of the community. If the factory is to pollute under these circumstances, it will have to compensate the community for the violation of their rights; it will have to buy from them the right to pollute. It will do so only if this is less expensive than stopping pollution—that is, if the value the community places on clean air is less than the cost of cleaning the air. In either case—the factory has the right to pollute or the community has the right to clean air—there will be a transaction that will lead to an efficient outcome. Pollution will be stopped if the cost of doing so is less than the value that the community places on clean air. So establishing property rights sets up a framework for a transaction between the affected parties that will lead to an outcome that is economically efficient.

Note that these two possible outcomes are both efficient economically but differ substantially in terms of the distribution of the costs and benefits involved. If the factory has the right to pollute and the community has to pay it to stop exercising that right, then there is a transfer from the community to the factory. In the other case, the factory has to buy from the community the right to continue polluting, and the transfer goes the other way. The point here is that we are creating new property rights where none existed previously, and these property rights have value. They enrich the party to whom they are assigned. If property rights are given to the community, the community is enriched by the gift of a right that the factory wishes to purchase; if they are given to the factory, it is enriched by a right that the community will pay to annul.

Pigou's insight has given rise to the dominant European policy approach in this field, namely, the use of corrective taxes and subsidies. Coase's has inspired the American approach of tradable permits and quotas, as used in the United States for controlling emissions of sulfur dioxide, lead additives, and water discharges. The key point in this approach is that before emitting a pollutant into the atmosphere, an entity must own the right to effect such an emission. Such a right is conveyed by the purchase of a tradable emission quota, or TEQ. The creation of these quotas establishes property rights in the atmosphere. If a business is forced to buy a quota before emitting a pollutant, then this also raises the private cost of pollution, in this case by the cost of the quota. Once again, private costs are changed so that they approach social costs. In fact, in a competitive quota market, private costs can be exactly equated to social costs by the inclusion of the costs of buying quotas:

PRIVATE COST + QUOTA PRICE = SOCIAL COST

How do we get the price of a quota to equal the private-social cost difference? By controlling the number of quotas: we can raise their price by lowering the number on the market, and we can lower their price by issuing more.

These two approaches, taxes and quotas, are formally equivalent in important ways, though not in all. A tradable quota system requires a polluter to buy a permit before polluting, thereby raising the private cost of pollution by an amount equal to the price of the permit. In this respect, it appears to the polluter like a tax. It imposes a tax equal to the price of a permit.

Both approaches are consistent with the "polluter pays" principle, which has been adopted by the OECD (Organization for Economic Cooperation and Development, consisting of North America, Western Europe, Australasia, and some recently industrialized countries). Compliance with this principle is widely viewed as a prerequisite for fairness in the management of pollution. In this respect the two approaches are similar. Nevertheless there are differences, which are associated with where the main policy uncertainties arise; these are explored below. There are also differences in the role of the government in each system: it plays a more central role, and of course raises revenue, under a tax regime.

Both taxes and tradable quotas are aimed at closing the gap between private and social costs and are very general in their range of application. There is another approach that may work in some situations. Recall Figure 2.3 above and that we refer to private-social cost differences as "external effects" because they are external to the market. This is represented in Figure 2.3, where ecosystem services are shown as being outside the market and as affecting society's welfare. The observation that these vitally important services are outside the market naturally prompts the question, Why? Why are the infrastructures upon which human societies depend outside the market? Can we perhaps find a solution by bringing them within the market, by extending the scope of the market, extending the scope of what we consider tradable, and establishing markets in which the services of natural systems are bought and sold?

This could be an attractive and effective solution because markets can be powerful forces for conservation. When important resources become scarce, their prices rise. This both promotes more conservative use and encourages the development of substitutes and the search for additional supplies. In the 1970s and 1980s, for example, high oil prices led to a drop in consumption and energetic searches for new sources, culminating in discoveries in the North Sea, the Gulf of Mexico, and Alaska. If the same discipline were to be applied to ecosystem services, many of our concerns would be reduced.

Figure 2.4 summarizes these ideas, building on Figure 2.3 by showing the scope of the market enlarged to include some ecosystem

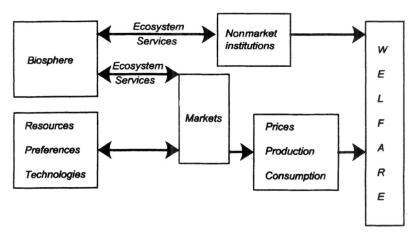

FIGURE 2.4. We need institutions to mediate the interactions between humans and the environment. To some degree markets can fill this role, but in some cases we need nonmarket institutions.

services and impacts on others controlled by other institutions. The next three chapters investigate the possibility of using markets for controlling our interactions with some of the Earth's basic life-support systems, by introducing markets for some of the services provided by natural ecosystems.

Illustrations

Let's now look at some possible applications of the issues addressed in this chapter[2] to see how incentives matter and how setting up the wrong incentives can damage the environment.

Consider first the conservation of Amazonian rainforests. This would have both costs and benefits; most people who have thought carefully about the issue believe that the benefits outweigh the costs. However, most of the costs would be borne by people who live in and around the forest; they include opportunity costs, costs of not being able to use the land for cash crops or for ranching, and of not being able to sell the timber. Some of the benefits, on the other hand, would accrue to everyone—to you, to me, to all human beings, because they are in the form of carbon sequestration and biodiversity support. Others accrue to people in Brazil, but not to those in the forest region; these are benefits from stream and flood control, regional climate control, and ecotourism, to name a few.

So in essence the local population pays the bill; the rest of us eat the meal. This is obviously not a stable situation: the bill payers will drop out. We can only expect the forest to be conserved if some of the benefits from conservation accrue to the bill payers.

This is a clear example of differences between the private and social benefits of conservation. The social benefits exceed the private, and consequently the incentives facing those who have to conserve the forests are too weak. The solution is in principle obvious: we must share with the local population who bears the costs of conservation some of the benefits that accrue to others but not to them.

---

2. This chapter has reviewed material that covers many complex issues in economics. For more general discussions of these, see *Principles of Economics* (Mankiw 1997); for an analysis in the environmental context, see *Environmental and Natural Resource Economics* (Tietenberg 1992).

This would strengthen their incentives to conserve and close the gap between private and social benefits from conservation. Later chapters will review mechanisms for doing this.

Another good illustration comes from a recent study of conservation on the island of Madagascar (Kremen, Niles, et al. 1999). The study looks at the costs and benefits of conserving the Masoala forest on Madagascar. Madagascar in general and this rainforest in particular contain a great number of unique species. Madagascar separated from the African continent relatively early in the evolutionary history of mammals and as a result contains species that are close to early lineages of many mammals. These include lemurs, which are thought to be close relatives of early primates. Elsewhere these animals have died out as a result of competition from their successors. Biologists therefore believe that the unique flora and fauna of Madagascar may make unique insights into the history of evolution possible.

Timber in this forest has considerable commercial value, and international timber companies constantly pressure the Malagasy government to grant logging concessions allowing them to cut the forest. There is also pressure on the forest from local populations. They practice slash-and-burn agriculture, cutting and burning the forest, growing a few crops until the fertility of the soil is destroyed (which happens very rapidly when rainforest is cut, as the soil in which it grows is thin and poor in nutrients), and then moving on. Kremen and her colleagues compared the returns of conserving this forest from three perspectives: that of the local population, that of the Malagasy government, and that of the world as a whole. The conservation policy considered involved some logging of the forest, done on a sustainable basis—in other words, selected logging of a few trees in a way that would minimize damage to the remaining forest and would be consistent with the forest's continued survival. It also involved the use of the forest as a source of nontimber products and the development of an ecotourism industry, together with assistance to the local community in developing settled agriculture. All of these activities could enhance the income of the local communities.

The conclusion of the study was that from the perspective of the local community, sustainable use of the type just described is more attractive than commercial logging. From the national government's point of view, the ranking is reversed: commercial logging is the most attractive because it brings in revenues from taxes and the sale of logging permits. From the global perspective, sustainable use is clearly the best option because of the value of carbon sequestration services performed by the forest. As ultimate decision-making power in this case rests with the central government, the forest will be preserved only if some of the value of the forest to the global community can be transformed into income for the Malagasy government. In other words, we need to bridge a gap between the private and social benefits of conservation, which in this case are the national and global benefits respectively. As the authors of the study note, Madagascar is one of the poorest countries on earth, so we cannot expect it to subsidize our consumption of fossil fuels.

Summary

The market is a marvelous device: it can achieve near-miracles in terms of organizing production and distribution efficiently. But it does not always work so benignly. In particular, there are important reasons that markets are not working well to manage our interactions with our ecological base. Some of the goods and services provided by our ecological base are outside the marketplace, as in the case of carbon sequestration. We can view this as a difference between the private and social costs and benefits of the economic activities that use the atmosphere. We can also think of the problem as a lack of property rights in the atmosphere. Several mechanisms might resolve this problem, including taxes and subsidies and the establishment of property rights. Another issue, to be addressed later, is the prevalence of public goods among ecosystem services. Rainforest conservation illustrates well that key ecosystem services are beyond the scope of the market, with the consequence that the incentives for conservation are inefficiently low.

Chapter 3

Markets and Ecosystems

It is now time to bring some of the general concepts of the previous chapters down to earth and consider how they apply in specific contexts. This chapter and the next two focus on three categories of ecosystems: those that act as watersheds, those that have the potential to attract tourists and provide a basis for ecotourism, and those that sequester carbon. The potential for markets to create positive incentives to protect vital ecosystems is greater in these cases than in many others, so they form a good starting point. They illustrate well the potential for modifying markets to reflect the proper values of important ecosystems, and they also illustrate some of the difficulties. As we shall see, some ecosystems can be simultaneously watersheds, sources of tourist revenues, and carbon sinks. There are other types of ecosystems whose services also have great market potential.

Watersheds

Freshwater is indisputably an essential commodity, so watersheds are a particularly crucial element of human social and economic infrastructure. Humans already use about 30 percent of the world's total accessible and renewable freshwater supplies (Postel, Daily, et al. 1996). In spite of this level of appropriation, we are short of clean freshwater. According to the United Nations Environment Program

(UNEP), 50 percent of people in developing countries suffer from one or more water-related diseases, and 80 percent of diseases in the developing world are caused by contaminated water (United Nations Environment Program 1999). The World Bank also rates inadequate access to freshwater as one of the main causes of illness in developing countries. Ensuring widespread access to reliable supplies of clean water is a major human priority.

To put the role of watersheds in context requires a digression on how we get our drinking water, something we in the United States typically take for granted. In some cases water is taken directly from rivers, as in the case of the Colorado River, which supplies parts of California. The catchment area for the Colorado River is vast, including a huge land area and the snowpacks in a region of the Rocky Mountains.

In other cases water comes from underground aquifers. Some of these refill regularly from rainfall, as do those that supply much of Long Island. Others contain water that has been there since the last glacial age, so-called fossil water. A good example is the Ogalala aquifer that serves much of the Great Plains states of the United States. Once exhausted, fossil water will not be replenished, and areas dependent on it will eventually need to look for alternative sources to satisfy their thirst.

The third method is water collected and channeled by hills and valleys into a valley and reservoir. This water can then be used directly to meet the needs of a nearby metropolitan area—New York, for example. Ninety percent of its water comes from the Catskills watershed, an area about ninety miles north and west of the city that channels water to the valley of the Hudson River. Likewise, many other large cities largely depend on a small number of nearby watersheds. Rio de Janeiro in Brazil depends on the basin of the Rio Paraibo do Sul and Buenos Aires in Argentina on the basin of the Rio Reconquista.

In the context of the goal of protecting the Earth's basic infrastructures, the conservation of watersheds is of great importance, partly because they are important in their own right, but also because they cover many regions of the Earth that are important as forests, which contribute to the carbon cycle, or as sources of biodiversity. Conservation of watersheds leads to the conservation of many areas that are important to other life-support systems of the planet.

To illustrate this point, the world's 106 largest watersheds cover 55 percent of the Earth's surface. About 3 billion people—about one-half of the world's population—live in them and, presumably, obtain their water from them. Between them they provide the only breeding places for over 3,000 species of fish and over 200 species of birds. They are probably important for conservation of plants, insects, and mammals as well, but the concentration of these species in large watersheds has not been studied.[1] Conserving even a small fraction of the Earth's watersheds could therefore make a major contribution to environmental conservation. And, as shall be discussed in what follows, market forces may be able to take us a long way in this direction.

Watersheds do far more than just collect water and route it to end-users. They perform two vital roles: stabilizing the flow of water and cleaning the water. Stabilization is valuable because rainfall provides a very uneven flow of water: its distribution over the annual climate cycle is usually poorly matched to the time pattern of consumers' water needs. Rain tends to fall in short, heavy bursts while water needs are spread more evenly over time. A watershed automatically compensates to some degree for this mismatch. The soil in a watershed is absorbent and soaks up water as rain falls on it, acting like a huge sponge. It then releases this water slowly over time, thereby stabilizing the pattern of stream flow from the watershed. Without this stabilization the pattern of water flow would match that of the rainfall. It would be uneven and characterized by sudden bursts. Figure 3.1 depicts this mechanism.

Trees play a central role in this living system. They not only hold soil in place, but their roots also interact with fungi and microorganisms in the soil to generate many of its most valuable properties. If the soil in the watershed erodes, then this service may be lost. An interesting example of these relationships was recently reported

---

1. This data is drawn from *Watersheds of the World* (Revenga, Murray, et al. 1998).

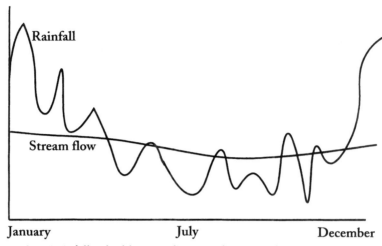

FIGURE 3.1. Rainfall is highly irregular over the year, whereas stream flow is more even because of the buffering and storage activities of soil in the watershed.

(Eckholm 1998). In the summer of 1998 China suffered some of the most severe floods in its history along the Yangtze valley. Inquiries attributed the severity of the floods in part to rainfall levels, but only in part. Rainfall was high but apparently not high enough to cause record floods. The balance was attributed to deforestation of the river's watershed by logging, which had caused soil erosion on the previously forested mountain slopes. After logging, a combination of heavy rain and steep slopes rapidly led to soil loss and in turn to a loss of the flow-control function of the watershed. Because the costs to downstream communities were unacceptable, in fall 1998 the Chinese government implemented a complete ban on all further logging in the watershed and an intensive program of reforestation.

Snowpacks, like watersheds, also play a central role in regulating water supplies, allowing water to flow gradually rather than in bursts corresponding to the pattern of precipitation. Snowpacks are typically important where the majority of a region's precipitation occurs in winter. In regions with high mountains snow remains frozen until late spring or summer, then melts over several months, generating stream flow at a time of year when water is much needed by agriculture but typically not available on an adequate scale from rainfall. In some regions a consequence of climate change may be earlier snowmelt, and therefore a change in the time pattern of flows in rivers, with more flow in the late winter and spring and less in summer. In effect climate change could compromise the watershed role of snowpacks by reducing their ability to hold water into the drier growing season.

The cleansing function of watersheds, their other vital role, occurs through processes in the soil and so is also dependent on soil health. Two things happen to water as it flows through soil: the soil acts as a filter for the slowly seeping water and traps small particles and organisms suspended in it. The slowness of the flow allows suspended particles to drop from the water into the soil. In addition to these natural filtration processes, microorganisms in the soil break down pollutants in the water and purify it in the process.

Soil is in fact a very complex entity, containing many chemicals and in addition an immense range of small organisms (Daily, Matson, et al. 1997). Soil organisms form communities that contribute to soil's fertility and its capacity to purify the water flowing through it. Anything that damages the functioning of the communities of organisms in the soil, such as pollution, can damage the ability of soil to play its cleansing role in a watershed.

Figure 3.2 shows schematically the two services—flow control and cleansing—that watersheds provide to communities.

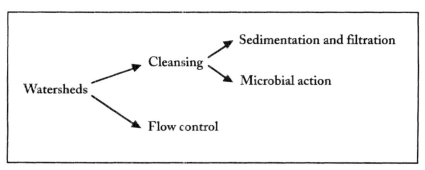

FIGURE 3.2. Watersheds control stream flow and cleanse water through microbial action and filtration.

Replaceability of Watershed Services

There are few possible substitutes for the flow-control role of watersheds, even in modern industrial communities. In many countries complex and extensive engineering projects have been developed to replace the flow-control function of watersheds; however, in most cases these have proven inadequate and indeed in some cases counterproductive. In the United States these have usually been undertaken by the Army Corps of Engineers and have involved truly massive investments. In the Chinese case cited above, the army and local communities had invested years in engineering projects aimed at controlling the increasingly uneven flow of the Yangtze River, to no avail.

The cleansing role is different; for this there are certainly some substitutes. Filtration plants can perform the filtration and sedimentation roles of soil, and chlorinating and other disinfectant processes can perform some of the additional purification roles, though these are not always complete replacements for natural processes. The most common form of treatment plant is a filtration plant, which removes small particles and microorganisms. Some particles are too small to be removed in this way but are nevertheless destroyed by bacteria in the watershed. The replacements may also have side effects that are lacking in natural processes. For example, the more powerful alternative to filtration is disinfecting by chlorine derivatives, which are thought by some to have possible side effects, including the formation of carcinogenic compounds. The replacements are also expensive, as shall be seen below.

In addition to their flow-control and cleansing functions, several important watersheds generate hydroelectric power for the communities they serve. A good example is the watershed for Rio de Janeiro, the basin of the Rio Paraibo do Sul, which flows inland of Rio. The river provides all the drinking water for about 18 million people and in addition provides 90 percent of the electricity used in Rio, which comes from hydropower. So it is clearly a major public utility for one of the world's largest cities. In a case like this one the analogy with infrastructure is clear and compelling. The watershed provides foundations for two vital utility systems, electricity and water.

Indeed, of all the natural ecosystems that support human soci-

eties, watersheds most closely resemble conventional economic infrastructure. They link directly to a critical item of urban infrastructure,
the water supply system, which may also be critical to the operation
of hydropower systems. Watersheds are often biologically important
areas so that their conservation may in such cases contribute to the
goal of biodiversity conservation. The basin of the Rio Paraibo do
Sul is also the location of a part of the Mata Atlantica, one of the
remaining fragments of the original Brazilian coastal rainforest. At
the time of European settlement this forest ran along the entire
Brazilian coast, although 97 percent of the forest has now been
destroyed. This forest is biologically quite unique: there are plants
and animals there that are found nowhere else in the world, including the recently discovered golden lion tamarin, a unique primate. So
conservation of this area would contribute greatly to the conservation of biological diversity, as well as to the conservation of the utilities of Rio.

The Catskill Watershed

A good illustration of the economic importance of a watershed is
provided by an analysis of the Catskill watershed of New York City.

Two watersheds serve New York City, one in the region of Croton and one in the Catskills, a range of hills about 3,000 feet high
and about 90 miles north and west of the city. The Croton reservoir
and watershed were the first to be used by the city and originally provided water that was drinkable without filtration or any form of
chemical treatment. Development near the reservoir changed this
rapidly: it led to the runoff of pollutants and to a great reduction in
the amount of soil available to act in a watershed role. Subsequently
New York invested in the Catskill watershed system, in a region that
was relatively sparsely populated. For many years the Catskills provided water of very high quality without filtration or chemical treatment. In fact, New York City water was known as some of the best
in the United States; in the 1930s and 1940s it was bottled and sold
in other cities, such was its reputation. It was the equivalent of Evian
or Perrier today.

In the 1990s the situation changed: water from the Catskills
region fell in quality to the point where the EPA warned the city that

it would shortly have to construct a filtration plant. Capital costs were estimated in the range of $6–8 billion with annual operating costs on the order of $300 million, an immense sum even for a prosperous city. Contemplation of these costs rapidly led the city to inquire why a watershed that had functioned so well for decades was now beginning to fail.

Investigation showed that the main causes of the decline were development in the Catskills area and intensified agricultural use of land in and around the watershed. Local communities had expanded and city dwellers had built summer homes. Untreated sewage was leaking from sewage systems into the watershed, and rainstorms were also washing gasoline, fertilizers, and pesticides from surrounding lands into the soils. In addition, animals from surrounding farms were straying into the watershed and polluting the streams. Animal feces can contain the organisms that cause cryptosporidium, a dangerous disease that can be fatal.[2] The combination of pollutants was overwhelming the soil microbial communities responsible for cleaning the water as it percolated through. Hence the drop in the purity of the city's drinking water, a result of damage to its watershed. In this case the damage was slight; there had been no deforestation or soil erosion, so that much of the infrastructure of the watershed was still intact and the damage was clearly reversible.

New York faced a choice: repair the watershed or build and run a filtration plant. The latter was expensive. The other option came with a price, too: the cost of environmental restoration—the cost of preventing further damage to the watershed and allowing it to recover from that already inflicted. But the cost was far less than a filtration plant; city officials estimated it to be in the range of $1–1.5 billion. Even if they were in error by a factor of two, the answer was clear: repair the watershed. At that time the commissioner of the city's Department of Environmental Protection commented, "All filtration does is solve a problem. Preventing the problem, through watershed protection, is faster, cheaper, and has lots of other bene-

---

2. In fact, an outbreak in Milwaukee in 1993 left 103 dead.

fits. Adding up the costs and benefits, watershed protection was not a difficult decision" (Trust for Public Lands 1997).

In 1997 the city floated an environmental bond issue with the intent of using the proceeds to restore the functioning of the Catskills watershed. Restoration actions to date have been of several types. They include improving sewage treatment in the watershed by installing new systems and improving old ones. They also include buying some 100,000 acres of land in and around the watershed to prevent development and to control agricultural use. In addition, the city used some of the money to purchase conservation easements from existing landowners whose land it did not buy outright.

Some of the measures have contributed additional income to farmers. One of these involves paying farmers to not grow crops or graze cattle along the banks of streams feeding the watershed. Payments are in the range of $100 to $150 per acre. The intention is to prevent a significant source of pollution—runoff of fertilizers, weed-killers, and pesticides. Keeping animals out of the streams also reduces the risk of cryptosporidium. Neither filtration nor chlorination can remove the organisms that cause this disease. One of the participants in the negotiations commented that society has to arrange that farmers in the region are paid to produce environmental benefits as well as food. As agriculture is one of the main sources of human pressure on the environment, this is an important point, one to which we will return in Chapter 8.

An important aspect of the New York story is that by improving sewage systems in the Catskills, by initiating other measures to reduce pollution there, and by buying conservation easements, New York City has improved the Catskills community's quality of life and injected a considerable amount of income into the region. In so doing it has provided some financial compensation to area residents and given them a direct financial stake in the conservation. This is analogous to Coase's model of the resolution of external effects discussed in the previous chapter. That is, in the case of a factory polluting a neighborhood, the introduction of property rights leads to bargaining between the two parties that corrects the inefficiency. Here, bargaining between the city and the polluters of the watershed leads the city to compensate the polluters in return for reduced pollution. In addition, legislative action by the State of New York strengthened the city's property rights by facilitating its use of compulsory purchase mechanisms.

It is too soon to know whether these actions have been sufficient to restore the watershed to its initial quality. However, it seems very likely that for less than $2 billion the watershed can be restored fully, at a saving relative to a technological fix of at least $4 billion—perhaps as much as $10 billion if operating costs are included. In fact, the restored watershed is probably a superior system to the filtration plant that was anticipated.

Taking all these issues into consideration, it appears that watershed conservation and repair are economically by far the most attractive water provision options open to a city. This is the conclusion reached some time back by professionals in the water management field. For example, in 1991, the *American Water Works Association Journal* observed: "The most effective way to ensure the long-term protection of water supplies is through land ownership by the water supplier and its cooperative public jurisdictions" (Trust for Public Lands 1997). Many urban areas other than New York City have now followed this path.

The Sterling Forest

In 1996 New Jersey decided to make watershed conservation a central part of its water strategy. A part of this new strategy was an agreement to ensure the conservation of Sterling Forest, an important watershed on the New York–New Jersey state border that was previously scheduled for residential development. The arrangement was similar to that in the Catskills, with much of the forest purchased by the state or conservation groups and a small part set aside for development. Again, interesting economic comparisons can be made. A new filtration plant to serve central New Jersey would have cost $112 million, whereas buying 17,000 acres of Sterling Forest cost $64 million. The forest will provide water to a larger community. Another illustration is the case of Gunnison, Colorado. This small but rapidly growing town recently went to some lengths to purchase a ranch located on top of the aquifer that provides the community's water. The reason? To ensure that the use of the ranchland did not in any way pollute the aquifer.[3]

In the United States the practice of watershed conservation is growing because of its economic logic. The United States is not alone here; the trend is growing internationally. In a recent essay Reid (1998) cites the following examples:

- La Tigra National Park in Honduras provides the capital city Tegucigalpa with 40 percent of its drinking water at a cost of about 5 percent of the next-largest source.
- Guatopo National Park in Venezuela provides 2,000 liters per second of high-quality drinking water to Caracas; $25 million has been spent buying out timber interests in the area.
- In Venezuela the Caroni River basin is the catchment area for 95 percent of the country's present and planned hydropower, which will provide 72 percent of the country's electric power needs.

South Africa provides an additional illustration: new proposed legislation identifies the management of watershed areas as critical to sustainable use of water and encourages land-use planning in these areas (see Revenga, Murray, et al. 1998).

Although economic arguments have contributed to the conservation of watersheds, it is interesting and important to note that it has been effected largely by political rather than economic institutions. Markets, our main economic institutions, have not played a leading role to date. In the New York case, capital markets were used to raise funds for conserving the watershed, and markets were of course used in purchasing land for watershed conservation. But the market was not the main driver of the conservation process; this was a political process. Could this have been different? Could matters have been so arranged that market forces initiated and were the main drivers of the transaction? This question matters because markets are always operating in search of profit opportunities. They are relentless in detecting and pursuing them. Political processes involving state agen-

---

3. For more details, see *Protecting the Source: Land Conservation and the Future of America's Drinking Water* (Trust for Public Lands 1997).

cies and special bond issues, as in the New York and New Jersey cases, are complex and fragile and one-off events. We cannot rely on processes of this type for all the watershed conservation that may be needed. Indeed, in many cases cities will not have New York's ability to borrow on global capital markets. We need to know whether there is a framework within which watershed conservation—and conservation generally—could be supported or even initiated by regular commercial forces, rather than by high-level political action. This requires thinking about securitization and privatization.

Securitization

Securitization involves issuing tradable contracts, called *securities,* which entitle their owners to a portion of the benefits from a venture. In exchange for the securities, investors contribute the capital needed for the venture. In effect they invest in the venture and receive a share of the benefits in return. Securitization is a technique extensively used for attracting investors. When venture capitalists invest in a new business, the enterprise is being securitized. When the same firm is floated on the stock exchange, this process is being taken further. It is no exaggeration to say that securitization is at the heart of capitalism.

In the environmental area, securitization is already used for investments in energy efficiency. In these cases, the securities entitle their owners to a specified fraction of the savings from improved energy efficiency in a building. Typically the investments are issued for retrofitting buildings with more energy-efficient heating, ventilating, and air-conditioning systems. The U.S. Department of Energy has developed a standard protocol for estimating the savings from enhanced energy efficiency, and several financial agencies are willing to accept the estimates as collateral for loans (Kats, Kumar, et al. 1999). The securities are tradable and can be sold even before the savings are realized. This financing method makes investment in energy efficiency attractive to the investing public and institutions, and it does not imply any transfer of ownership of the underlying asset.

Let's look at a hypothetical example of how securitization can work in other types of conservation projects. In the case of the New

York watershed, investors would have been investing in "watershed securities," which would entitle them to a fraction of the cost savings resulting from watershed restoration. The city could pay investors for the use of their capital through a "watershed savings account" into which it paid a fraction of the costs avoided by not having to build and run a filtration plant (Chichilnisky and Heal 1998).

What advantages does securitization have for municipalities? What gains would securitization bring, relative to what actually happened? The purpose of securitization is to attract financing without using the credit of the city itself. Under the scenario just described, the city itself would not have to borrow. Investors would invest directly in watershed restoration, not via a city bond issue. This could be an important point for a municipality with an active investment agenda and many other uses competing for funds. It could also be a valuable technique in developing countries whose metropolitan areas often do not have credit ratings comparable to New York's and so do not have access to capital markets. The EPA recently estimated the cost of providing adequate water treatment facilities in the United States by 2020 at $138.4 billion (Trust for Public Lands 1997). The massive order of magnitude of this sum underlines the importance of taking watershed protection off the list of projects to be funded by municipal funds, which will be stretched by many other socially important demands in the coming decades.

Privatization

The securitization scenario takes government out of the picture as far as obtaining financing is concerned. But it remains the prime mover of the project. One could in principle take the introduction of market forces another step and further reduce government's role. In regions where local governments are corrupt, incompetent, or simply unreliable, this could be an essential condition to moving ahead.

To see how privatization might work, imagine a corporation managing the restoration of New York City's watershed. Most likely this would be a regulated private corporation, perhaps resembling in some respects a public utility such as the local phone or power company. It might be called the Catskills Watershed Corporation (CWC). CWC has the right to sell to New York City the services of the

Catskills ecosystem, the provision of water meeting EPA standards. Ownership of this right would enable it to raise capital from capital markets, to be used for meeting the costs of conservation. This process is called *privatization.*

Privatization requires some regulation because the corporation would be a natural monopoly and regulating prices would be appropriate. It would also be reasonable to place some restrictions on the modifications that the corporation could make to the natural ecosystems in the watershed area.

This concept is not far-fetched; in fact, it is close to what is happening in countries where water supplies have been privatized. In the United Kingdom, France, and a number of developing countries, private companies are now in the business of supplying water (for example, Generale des Eaux). Initially these companies primarily provided pipeline services moving water from its sources to consumers. They were not responsible for the water sources themselves. A few years of experience convinced them that whatever their legal position, they would be viewed as responsible when the sources proved inadequate to meet demand, and they were responsible for the quality of the water supplied. Pollution of a watershed could therefore impose high costs on them: it could force them into constructing treatment plants, just as it almost did for New York. If they were responsible for delivering water of a certain quality, then it made economic sense for them to have control over any watersheds on which they were dependent.

Under the same logic commercial water suppliers in the United States and, to a greater extent, elsewhere are increasingly seeking control over watersheds, if necessary by buying them. The preferred, less costly strategy is to try to have the local government declare the watershed regions conservation zones. An interesting example of this trend is provided by a recent attempt to privatize the water supply of Lima, Peru's capital city. A number of companies were invited to submit proposals for privatization of Lima's water supplies. All made it clear that they would not be able to run the water supply system unless development in the watershed region were restricted. The watershed region was then the subject of proposals for commercial development. When the government stated that it was not able to guarantee the integrity of the watershed, it found that no companies were willing to tender proposals for privatization.

There are many further examples of financial incentives operating to conserve watersheds. The city of Portland, Maine, annually spends almost three-quarters of a million dollars on watershed conservation programs. These have enabled it to receive a filtration waiver from the Evironmental Protection Agency (EPA) and avoid the expenditure of $25 million for construction of a filtration plant. Portland, Oregon, spends just under $1 million annually and as a result avoids the need to spend about $200 million on treatment plants. In Connecticut water companies have acquired more than 130,000 acres of land around watersheds, leading to large reductions in water-monitoring costs. In 1989 Rhode Island imposed a water-use surcharge of 2.59 cents per 100 gallons, about one-quarter of which is spent on land acquisition around watersheds. Through this program the city of Providence has spent $16 million to buy land around watersheds.

Recent regulations in the United States have created strong incentives to expand the scope of watershed protection. About 700 of the nation's 10,000 surface-water systems are unfiltered, with about 130 legally avoiding filtration through ownership of the source. The remainder are under pressure from the EPA to install filtration plants. Many of these could benefit economically from watershed protection. Reid has calculated that within the continental forty-eight states an extension of economically justified watershed protection could lead to protection of 10 percent of their land area.[4]

Similar moves are occurring farther afield. In Venezuela, the Rio Caroni basin is the catchment area for 95 percent of the country's present and planned hydropower developments. The utility that runs the projects has lobbed hard for conservation of the basin and a ban on commercial agriculture there. In this case the ecosystem service it wants to conserve is the flow-control function; the utility is also concerned that deforestation will lead to siltation of the dam (Reid 1998).

---

4. For details, see Reid 1998 and Trust for Public Lands 1997.

Markets and Watersheds

All these examples lead to an interesting, perhaps surprising, conclusion: once we introduce market forces into the provision of water, they tend to push us farther down the road to conserving the natural systems on which water resources depend. The reason is clear: natural systems provide vital infrastructure for water companies. The companies have a strong financial incentive to work for conservation and, if necessary, to pay for it. So privatizing water supply creates a commercial lobby for conservation.

How does this analysis relate to the issues raised in Chapter 2 on the market's performance? In particular, how does the discussion of externalities and public goods apply? Clearly damage to a watershed, either by development or by pollution, is a harmful external effect inflicted on the community. Equally clearly, watersheds provide important services that are not mediated by the market and are external to the market—they are external effects in a classical sense. The situation is exactly as shown in Figure 2.3 in the previous chapter, although the concept of public good is less relevant in this case: water is a commodity that is rival and excludable. If I do not pay for connection, I can in principle be excluded from consumption, and if I use a certain volume of water, then you cannot use it. At least, if I drink it, then you cannot. Some lower-value uses may be nonrival—for example, several industrial plants might in principle be able to use the same water for cooling.

So the main issue in the case of water supply is externalities. In the New York City example, the externalities were corrected by establishing property rights in the watershed, with New York obtaining certain property rights in the Catskills so that it could take steps to stop polluting activities in and around the watershed. Recall in the previous chapter that "externalities" were interpreted in two different ways: as differences between the private and social costs or benefits of an action and as an absence of property rights. The two solutions that emerged naturally from these interpretations are (1) to close the gap between private and social costs or benefits through the use of taxes or subsidies, and (2) to establish property rights so that the external effects at issue can be brought within the framework of a transaction. The latter is the way the Catskill situation was handled: New York City obtained the right to purchase some land around the watershed by use of eminent domain legislation. In other cases it bargained to obtain an agreement to reduce pollution and restrict development. These agreements typically involved paying landowners to accept restrictions on the use of their land but paying less than would have been needed to purchase the land outright.

Another mechanism used, although on a much smaller scale, was paying farmers to stop growing crops or grazing animals on land next to streams that feed the watershed. Here we have a classic example of the other approach to external effects, namely, bringing private and social costs and benefits into equality. The social benefits of allowing land alongside streams to lie fallow exceed the private benefits. In fact, there are no private benefits: the farmer gains nothing from fallow land. But there are social benefits: society gains from protecting the quality of its water. Paying farmers to hold land fallow increases the private benefits and aligns them with the social benefits.

Securitization and commercial management of the watershed would be a step further in the direction of using the market: it would bring a nonmarket commodity, the service of the watershed, within the scope of the market. This is a natural extension of the Coasian solution of introducing property rights. In this case it would be relatively straightforward—and indeed it is already happening to some degree—as water is a good for which individuals or municipalities are willing to pay. They are willing to pay for quality as well as quantity, which in effect puts a price on the water management and purification services provided by a watershed. It generates an indirect demand, what economists call a *derived demand*, for watersheds. The possibility of replacing some of the functions of a watershed with a filtration plant puts an upper limit on what would make sense to spend on restoring the watershed, of the order of $8 billion in the New York case. This is, of course, only from the water management and purification perspective. Society may value the watershed for other reasons as well; in the New York case, the Catskills are a popular recreational area, and society has a substantial willingness to pay for this use in addition to watershed services.

Note that we have focused here mainly on land-use threats to the roles of watersheds—threats posed by residential and industrial development or by agriculture. Other threats are less local and less readily countered. Climate change could alter precipitation patterns and change the availability of water to watersheds, threatening their functions in a more insidious manner. This is a problem that could not be countered by local actions alone and would require global responses. Diffuse pollution such as acid rain or the transportation of nitrates released from fertilizers could also threaten watersheds by altering the acidity of the water and soils, thereby changing the basic chemical and biological processes that allow them to operate. None of these threats to the system's functional integrity can be removed by local action in the region of the watershed; all may originate many miles away.

Summary

Watersheds are the prime example of ecosystems as public utilities, as natural infrastructure to our built systems. Many biologically important ecosystems and regions contribute to the functioning of watersheds, which are among the most essential infrastructures on the planet. They do well at no cost two things that we cannot do, or can do only at great cost: control stream flow and purify water. In both roles they have immense economic value. Their value in these roles often exceeds any value they might have as agricultural land or residential developments, so that it is economically rational to conserve them. Yet their economic value is often unnoticed, mainly because water is not priced. Making more use of market forces in the allocation of water will make the value of watersheds more obvious and enlist economic forces in their conservation. It may be possible to privatize the conservation and management of watersheds by giving corporations the right to manage them and sell the water they provide. National and international priority for watershed conservation, with seed funding from the World Bank and similar agencies, could serve to prime the pump in this endeavor.

Chapter 4

Ecotourism

Tourism is one of the world's largest industries, possibly the largest in the world in terms of value of output. It may generate as much as 7 percent of all employment, 5 percent of all income, and 8 percent of all exports worldwide (Lanza and Pigliaru 1999; Sinclair 1998). It is also growing rapidly in value, by at least 10 percent annually (Ecotourism Society 1998). The value of international tourism exceeds $400 billion. Recent estimates suggest that about $150–250 billion of the total is related to nature and the desire to visit areas of natural beauty and integrity.

We can think of ecotourism as tourism driven by a desire to see unusual and distinctive natural environments. This is a simplification and avoids some of the finer points that arise in trying to distinguish between different varieties of tourism—for example, nature tourism, wildlife tourism, and so forth.[1]

Tourism underpins the economies of many areas. In several developing countries that are rich in biodiversity and natural resources,

---

1. For a detailed discussion of ecotourism and an attempt at defining it, see *Ecotourism and Sustainable Development: Who Owns Paradise?* (Honey 1999). See also the "Ecotourism Statistical Fact Sheet" (Ecotourism Society 1998) for attempts to define and measure wildlife and nature tourism and a review of how they relate to ecotourism.

international tourism is a major source of foreign exchange. For Costa Rica and Kenya, for instance, international tourism brings on the order of one-third of total foreign exchange revenues. The same is true for many countries in southern Africa. In Kenya, ecotourism generates revenues comparable to those from its main export crops, coffee and tea. For these countries, the earnings from ecotourism are a return on the preservation of their unique ecosystems. People visit these countries because of their flora and fauna, in particular because of what ecologists call their "charismatic megafauna," by which they mean large and appealing animals such as lions or giraffes or brightly colored birds. Conserving the natural ecosystems that support these animals can bring a substantial economic return in the form of tourist revenue.

When people pay to visit a region as ecotourists, they are paying for an ecosystem service. The good being sold is the ability to see and experience natural ecosystems containing attractive and unusual animals and plants. You may recall Daily's definition of ecosystem services quoted in Chapter 1, which included "provision of aesthetic beauty and intellectual stimulation that lift the human spirit." To some extent that is what is being transacted in ecotourism. Visitors find the animals and plants a beautiful and uplifting source of wonder. Seeing them can give us new insights into who we are, into what is important to us, and into how the world works. One might say this captures the real meaning of recreation: it is the opportunity to reinvent or re-create ourselves through new experiences and insights and through reflection on our origins and the overall scheme of which we are a part. For many people natural environments are important in this process. This is not a life-support service in a strict sense, but it is a service that is critical to the quality of life.

It is important economically that by selling this recreational service, countries whose natural environments play a role in planetary life-support systems may be able to earn a return on their conservation. Conserving the Amazonian forests is probably central to several important planetary and regional life-support systems. The next two chapters discuss how the economic value of some of these may be realized. The willingness of affluent people from industrial countries to pay to visit some of the remarkable phenomena to be found in Amazonia represents an additional incentive to conserve rather than destroy the region and so continue its contribution to planetary carbon and hydrological cycles.

Generally regions where ecotourism is most successful are those with a high degree of biodiversity and endemism. Biodiversity is a topic to which we shall return; as noted earlier, it denotes the extent of a region's variation in species. Endemic species are those specific to an area and found nowhere else. We will see later that biodiversity and endemism are characteristics that may be important for reasons quite unconnected to the possibility of generating tourist business. Regions with these characteristics may be just those it is most important to preserve in order to keep intact the knowledge and genetic potential inherent in biodiversity.

One of the most powerful examples of how ecotourism can work comes from South Africa, in the form of the Conservation Corporation, or ConsCorp, a company started as a private venture. It capitalized on the demand for ecotourism and hunting. This demand is such that land annually yielding $25 per hectare through ranching and $70 per hectare through farming can yield between $200 and $300 per hectare as part of a reserve managed for tourism or hunting. (A hectare is about 2.5 acres.) In South Africa ConsCorp contracts with landowners to incorporate their land in its reserves; it does not buy the land outright. Landowners have to maintain their land in accordance with tightly specified regulations and to stock it with specified animals. ConsCorp manages the business part of the operation, bringing in tourists and hunters, building facilities, and providing guides and vehicles. To date it has restored several hundred thousand hectares of farmland to something like their original ecosystems.

An interesting detail is that the presence of lions will add about 30 percent to the revenues from an area, so that the incentive to restock them is great.[2] But if lions, at the apex of the food chain, are to be present, the rest of the food chain—what lions eat, what the lions' food eats, and so on—must be present as well. Thus there is a strong economic incentive to do a thorough job of restoring the orig-

---

2. Personal communication, Craig Packer, professor, Department of Ecology and Evolution, University of Minnesota.

inal ecosystem from the alterations made by agricultural use. This is in fact clear from the very explicit rules used by the ConsCorp, whose articles of association for a specific reserve state that its aims are

> to promote and conserve endemic wildlife within the confines of the area . . . ; to establish the Reserve as a sanctuary in perpetuity for endemic wildlife and habitat so as to ensure sustainable resource utilization . . . ; to endeavor to increase the area of the Reserve; and to maximize the long term economic and ecological value of the properties.

Landowners even agree not to keep any domestic animals, dogs and cats included. An interesting quote from a South African writer (Capstick, cited in Anderson 1996) captures some of what is happening in this movement:

> The interesting thing is that untold hundreds of thousands of hectares and morgen that even a few years ago were scrub grazing for a mixture of game and cattle have now been entirely allocated to game. Why? Economics, as always. Game pays its own way, eats nearly anything, is more resistant to disease and predators and generally produces a higher and better use for the land. . . . Even the old enemies become assets to the farmer who switches from cattle to game. One friend of mine used to lose as many as thirty calves a season to leopards. . . . Now those same leopards are worth a cool $3,000 to $4,000 to sport hunters, not a bad trade-off for animals that caused a liability of well over ten grand and had to be poisoned! Tell me, is that bad for leopards?

An interesting aspect of the situation in South Africa is the law applied to mobile animals: if they are on your land and you capture them, then they are yours. This legal framework originated in Namibia in 1967 and then spread to Zimbabwe and South Africa (Freese 1999). It's important in terms of the demand for animals needed to restock reserves like ConsCorp's—a need that has created a market for wildlife and so a value for captured animals. Farmers finding animals on their land would once have shot or poisoned them because of the damage they did to crops and structures. Now they are more likely to capture them, probably with the assistance of professionals, and sell them at wildlife auctions at which the parks and preserves restock. Game is now an asset rather than a liability. In many other African countries this "rule of capture" for wild animals does not apply: if you find an elephant on your land, you cannot capture and sell it, so it remains a liability, damaging crops and structures and having no redeeming asset-like characteristics.

The conservation impact of ecotourism, including sport hunting, has already been large and positive in southern Africa and is likely to be developed further. In Angola, Botswana, Kenya, Malawi, Mozambique, Namibia, South Africa, Tanzania, Zambia, and Zimbabwe, about 18 percent of all land is now devoted to wildlife (Cumming 1990a; Cumming 1990b; Cumming and Bond 1991). Some of this takes the form of national parks and other areas protected by the state, but an increasing amount is privately owned land devoted to "game ranching," the term used for raising wildlife commercially. The aim of game ranching is almost always either tourism or hunting, or a combination of the two.

Figure 4.1 shows how the land devoted to wildlife in Zimbabwe

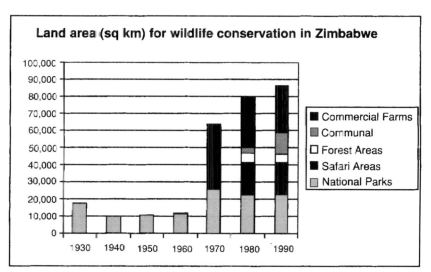

FIGURE 4.1. The growth of land devoted to wildlife conservation in Zimbabwe. Note that most of the growth comes from safari areas and commercial farms. Data drawn from Bond (1993), Cumming (1990a and b), and Cumming and Bond (1991).

has increased over time and how it breaks down between different forms of ownership. State-organized conservation areas provide a solid basis for wildlife conservation, with the growing commercial operations more than doubling the total land devoted to wildlife. Eighteen percent of the land area of these countries is not only a huge amount of land but also a striking increase of the amount of land available for wildlife only one or two decades ago. Some of the commercial operations are corporations, such as the Conservation Corporation and Wilderness Safaris Pty. Others are formed by ranchers who have converted their land to game ranching and then auctioned the right to run tourist or hunting safaris over their land to tour operators. In many cases individual farms are too small to be competitive, so several owners pool their land, removing the fences that previously separated their farms and replacing them with a common perimeter fence.

In Botswana, where commercial farming had less hold on the land than in many other countries of the region, most of the land used for ecotourism is on government-owned reserves. Typically these are large areas, tens of square miles in size. The government leases concessions to tour operators for fifteen years subject to performance reviews every five years. There are restrictions on the number of beds that can be operated on each concession, which is typically limited to about one per square mile.

Not only is game ranching a more profitable use of large areas of land than conventional agriculture, but it is also a more stable source of income, an important factor in its success. The reason is that the flora and fauna native to an area are more likely to be able to survive the vagaries of its weather than are imported species such as wheat and cattle. Dry years have less impact on earnings from ecotourism than on earnings from cattle or crops. Figures 4.2 and 4.3 show representative returns available from game ranching and from agriculture in three regions of Zimbabwe, in the first case as a return on investment and in the second as a return per hectare. The three regions are arid, semiarid, and wetlands.

Similar developments are occurring in Kenya, although not with the same degree of success. But the results tell the same story in terms of incentives: in the Laikipia region of Kenya ecotourism can bring

Financial returns to wildlife and cattle ranching in Zimbabwe

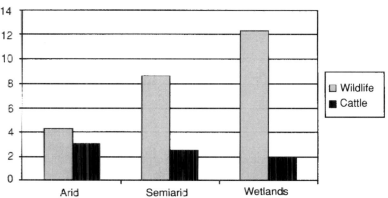

FIGURE 4.2. The returns on investment from raising wildlife and cattle in various regions of Zimbabwe. Data drawn from Bond (1993), Cumming (1990a and b), and Cumming and Bond (1991).

Returns per hectare from wildlife and cattle in Zimbabwe

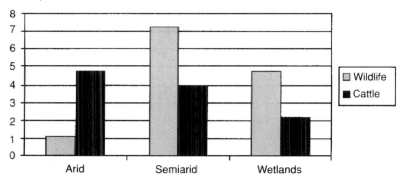

FIGURE 4.3. The returns per hectare from raising wildlife and cattle in various regions of Zimbabwe. Data drawn from Bond (1993), Cumming (1990a and b), and Cumming and Bond (1991).

$5 to $30 per hectare annually, compared with less than $2 per hectare for traditional livestock husbandry (Rubenstein 1993). In Kenya all the numbers are lower, partly because the ecosystems are less productive and probably also because the country has less infrastructure and is a less attractive destination for tourists.

Infrastructure is a prerequisite for successful ecotourism. International airports, roads, hotels and restaurants, and medical facilities need to be in place before tourism can take off. Political stability is another important element of the infrastructure that tourists seek in destination countries. Uganda had a thriving ecotourism industry until the mid-1970s, but fifteen years of political instability destroyed it. It is only slowly being reconstructed.

Another important difference between the southern African countries and Kenya and Uganda is in the directness of the links between wildlife conservation and the economic returns from conservation. As Chapter 2 observed, if the owners and managers of natural ecosystems are to have real incentives to conserve them, then the value that these systems provide to others must be reflected in the rewards to those who own and manage them. In the countries of southern Africa, this has generally been the case. Organizations like ConsCorp and concessions based on groups of farms take the trouble to ensure that a part of the returns from tourism goes directly to the landowners.

In several of the more northerly countries the government takes a large portion of tourist revenues, and then the balance goes not to individual landowners but to the community on whose land the tourism occurs, often in the form of investment in community infrastructures. The link between conservation and rewards is weaker, and consequently the incentives to conserve are also weaker. In countries where ecotourism is managed on this basis the attractions of more conventional agriculture appear greater and are harder to overcome. As one commentator explains, "The benefits of agropastoralism accrue directly to the individual, while the benefits from wildlife are essentially communal" (Bond 1993; Freese 1999, 92). This illustrates the point that the form of economic organization can affect the possibility of transforming the potential for conservation into reality. This transformation requires the right incentives. As already noted, the local community in the area to be conserved must share in the benefits from conservation. They certainly bear some, indeed most, of the costs, so without a share of the benefits they have nothing to gain from conservation. The benefits from pastoralism do accrue directly to the local community, so without a share of the gains from conservation, communities will not give up this lifestyle. Unfortunately, the governments of several African states have not understood this point.

Ecotourism is further developed, and better documented, in Africa than elsewhere. But it is nevertheless a significant force in other regions. The volume of nature-based tourism is growing rapidly in Central and South America (Honey 1999), and in regions of Asia the demand for photo and hunting safaris has led to significant increases in the populations of endangered species (Freese 1999, 197). Ecotourism is important even in the United States: in Texas landowners receive between $100 and $300 million in hunting leases each year, although it is not clear that this leads them to invest in conservation. Perhaps a more positive illustration is the revenue from duck-hunting licenses, which has been used to purchase some 4 million acres of wetlands for conservation purposes (Freese 1999, 198).

Of course, ecotourism need not be land-based. The beauty of coral reefs brings snorkelers and divers, who are drawn by the natural ecosystems around coral reefs. Consequently much tourism in the Caribbean and around the Great Barrier Reef in Australia is ecotourism, and much of the prosperity of these regions is a return on their natural ecosystems. But conservation of marine ecosystems is problematic. The coastal shelf is public property with open access. Consequently, there are no owners who, like the farm owners in Africa, have incentives to conserve and restock. Likewise there are no owners who can impose regulations preventing damage from overuse. This lack of property rights is a general hindrance to conservation of these marine ecosystems.

There is currently no prospect of the marine equivalent of game ranching, the conversion of agricultural to conservation uses. There may therefore be a case for privatizing coral reefs: giving a single group or company the exclusive right, for a limited period, to grant access and charge for snorkeling, diving, and fishing in a specified area. This group would then have a strong incentive to supervise use so as to prevent damage and ensure the continuing value of its property. Many of the threats to reefs, such as sewage, agricultural runoff, and global warming, would still be beyond their control, but they would at least have an incentive to lobby for their reduction and even to take legal action in furtherance of this goal where possible.

Summary

What can we conclude about the potential of markets for conserving the ecosystems that support appealing and charismatic flora and fauna? The evidence is very encouraging but not yet conclusive. It suggests that this is a direction to be explored carefully.

Ecotourism has momentum already. It is naturally a private market-based activity, so there is no need for privatization. Financial incentives appear to be working well and having a major impact. There are still some frictions that intelligent policy makers could reduce, such as the tenuous connection between tourist revenues and individual rewards on communal lands in Zimbabwe. Facilitating such changes should be an active concern of domestic and international agencies. Overall, the potential of market-based incentives for conserving both watersheds and the distinctive ecosystems that appeal to tourists seems great. Merely realizing this potential could make a real difference in the state of the Earth's life-support systems. But in fact we can probably go much further. As we shall see in the next chapter, carbon sequestration can also provide financial incentives for conservation, in this case of forests.

Chapter 5

Forests, Carbon, and Kyoto

Among all their other roles, forests are central to the global carbon cycle. Forests are major sinks of carbon, taking out of the atmosphere about 10^{15} grams of carbon each year, 14 percent of the total emitted by human activities. The roles of various sources and sinks of carbon in the global carbon cycle are depicted in Figure 1.1 on page 6. In a world concerned about climate change induced by increased greenhouse gases, this is an important service, potentially as valuable as any other the forest can provide.

The importance of the nontimber services provided by forests was recognized in a recent report drafted by the chief executives of timber companies at a meeting convened under the auspices of the World Bank. The report offers this vision of the forest company of the twenty-first century (World Bank 1998):

> The forest company of the 21st century will be in the business of managing renewable resources, selling a variety of non-timber services in addition to sustainably produced timber. Sale of these services can help finance and motivate conservation of natural forests. Forestry companies, environmental organizations, and those who enjoy forest benefits have a mutual interest in creating these markets, and should work together to realize this goal.

The same report offers a succinct statement of key economic issues, in much the same terms used here, but in this case applied to forests:

> Forests provide a wide variety of local, national, and global services, including carbon sequestration, biodiversity conservation, recreation, and watershed protection. These benefits, however, do not usually accrue to the forest owner or manager, who lacks both the incentives and the funds to maintain these services. In principle, if beneficiaries of these environmental services paid for them, forest owners would profit from maintaining standing forests, and incentives would shift from forest destruction to forest preservation.

This analysis provides a brief summary of many of the themes introduced in earlier chapters: incentives, external effects, and bringing private and social benefits into equality to correct inefficiencies. It also anticipates policy themes to which we will return in Chapter 8. In addition, the report identifies the services potentially marketable by the forest company of the twenty-first century. We have already looked in detail at the roles of forests as watersheds and sources of ecotourism. This chapter applies the ideas of earlier discussions to the carbon sequestration role of forests; the next chapter addresses their role in biodiversity support and the potential of non-timber forest products.

Forest Services as Public Goods

In terms of economics, a central feature of carbon sequestration is that it is a public good. This means, as noted in Chapter 2, that the composition of the atmosphere is similar for all of us. If the climate remains unchanged because atmospheric composition is unaltered, then it does so for us all. Hence there is no rivalry in the consumption of benefits from climate conservation. The stabilization of the existing climate regime is also nonexcludable, the other characteristic of a public good. The point is that any group that acts to reduce climate change cannot exclude others from benefiting from its actions. If the European Union cuts back greenhouse gas emissions but the United States does not, the United States gains as much as the European Union—an illustration of the classical free-rider problem.

There is one additional and nonclassical aspect of atmospheric composition from the public-good perspective: it is privately produced. The traditional examples of public goods—defense, law and order, broadcasting—are all produced by a central authority or, at least in the case of broadcasts, at a small number of locations. In contrast, the composition of the atmosphere is influenced by every person and every business on the planet. There are 6 billion human producers of carbon dioxide (not to mention many billions of livestock producers), and the number is growing daily. And the removal of carbon dioxide through carbon sequestration is determined in part by the forest cover of the planet, again something affected by millions of individual choices about land use and forest clearing. So CO_2 is injected into and removed from the atmosphere as the outcome of billions of decentralized and independent decisions by private households for heating, transportation, and land use, by corporations for these and other reasons, all outside the government's sphere. Governments can influence them, but only indirectly, through regulations or incentives.[1]

In other words, carbon sequestration by forests is a public good that is privately produced. What does that imply for the management of forests? And how can we use markets as a mechanism providing incentives for carbon sequestration? As the timber company chief executives cited above noted, we clearly have to find some system for closing the gap between public and private benefits from forest growth.

Markets for Carbon Sequestration

The Kyoto Protocol, formally the Kyoto Protocol of the United Nations Framework Convention on Climate Change (UNFCCC), is

---

1. The same holds true for other atmospheric pollutants. Sulfur dioxide is produced by the home-heating and power-generation choices of people the world over. Ozone-depleting chlorofluorocarbons are used in household refrigerators and air conditioners.

an agreement reached in Kyoto in December 1997 between the members of the UNFCCC. These include most countries in the world, so this is effectively a global agreement. The essence of the agreement is a set of coordinated moves to reduce the production of greenhouse gases and to encourage the conservation and extension of carbon sinks, systems that remove carbon from the atmosphere. Forests, as we have remarked, are prime entries in this category. One notable feature of the Kyoto Protocol is an agreement to use tradable emission permits as one of the mechanisms for controlling the production of greenhouse gases.

This aspect of the Kyoto Protocol—the use of tradable permits—is linked to an interesting provision that may lead to a mechanism for closing the gap between the private and social returns of forestry. But before going over it in detail, let's look at it and other mechanisms for controlling the provision of privately produced public goods, such as atmospheric composition.

The U.S. Sulfur Dioxide Market

The tradable permit system adopted in the Kyoto Protocol was first used on a significant scale in the United States as a result of the 1990 Clean Air Act. This act introduced a system of tradable emission permits for sulfur dioxide, a gas emitted by the combustion of fossil fuels containing sulfur. On dissolving in moisture in the atmosphere, sulfur dioxide forms sulfurous acid, which, in combination with rainfall, leads to acid rain.

The regime introduced by the 1990 Clean Air Act operates approximately as follows. The EPA sets a limit on the amount of sulfur dioxide to be emitted in the United States and issues a number of permits, each giving its owner the right to emit 1 ton of sulfur. Sulfur may not be emitted without ownership of a permit. Permits can be traded on an organized market; transactions in the sulfur dioxide market are conducted through the Chicago Board of Trade.

This regime attains two goals. First, it limits the production of sulfur dioxide to the total number of permits issued by the EPA. Second, it ensures that reduction of sulfur emissions occurs at least cost. Why is this? Suppose that you and I both run electric utilities burning coal. Permits to emit sulfur cost $100 per ton. As shown in Fig-

---

Permit Price $100

Abatement cost $80   Abate and sell (or don't buy) permit

Abatement cost $120   Emit and use (or buy) permit

FIGURE 5.1. If permits cost $100, those whose abatement costs are less have an incentive to abate and avoid buying a permit, and those whose costs are higher will buy a permit and so incur a cost of emission of $100, which could be avoided by abatement. Therefore, both types have an incentive to abate emissions.

ure 5.1, it costs me $80 to reduce my emissions by a ton: your costs are $120. What will happen? Clearly even if I have a permit, I should reduce sulfur emissions. This will cost me $80 and will let me sell my permit for $100, a gain of $20. If I did not initially have a permit, the case is even clearer: spending $80 saves me from having to buy a permit for $100.

What about you? If you own a permit, you will use it, foregoing the $100 you could get from its sale but saving the $120 it would cost you to abate emissions. And if you do not own a permit, you are clearly better off buying one for $100 and emitting a ton of sulfur than abating emissions by 1 ton at a cost of $120. So in all cases, I will abate my emissions and you will not: the cutback in pollution occurs at the firm whose abatement costs are lowest.[2]

A market for emission permits, such as the sulphur dioxide market in the United States or the market in greenhouse gases proposed by the Kyoto Protocol, is a mechanism for deciding how best to attain a target reduction in emissions. It is not a way of deciding what that reduction should be—it does not tell us how to pick the target. In the terms used in Chapter 2, this is a Coasian solution to the problem posed by the emission of greenhouse gases. We are establishing property rights where none existed previously and then

---

2. For a more comprehensive review of the economics of markets for tradable permits, see the introductory chapters of *Environmental Markets* (Chichilnisky and Heal 2000).

distributing them to the participating countries. In the United States the 1990 Clean Air Act assigns this role to the EPA; and if the Kyoto Protocol is implemented, the UNFCCC will presumably play a similar role or establish a body to play that role. Creation of property rights is established by forbidding the emission of greenhouse gases without the possession of a permit. Something that was previously open to everyone is now open only to those who have bought the right to it.

The Kyoto Protocol

The Kyoto Protocol assigns to markets the role of deciding how best to attain a target reduction. The political processes leading up to the protocol chose a target reduction in carbon emissions and a date for its attainment. The following list summarizes some of the key provisions of the protocol, as far as they are relevant to this chapter:[3]

1. Industrial countries are to reduce emissions by 5 percent relative to 1990 levels by 2008 to 2012.
2. Net emissions are what count in point 1 above. These are defined as "net changes in greenhouse gas emissions by sources and removals by sinks resulting from direct human-induced land use change and forestry activities, limited to afforestation, reforestation and deforestation since 1990, measured as verifiable changes in carbon stocks in each commitment period" (Article 3, point 1).
3. "Demonstrable progress" should have been made toward these targets by 2005 (Article 3, point 2).
4. There is a provision for trading emissions reductions: "Any emission reduction units, or any part of any assigned amount, which a Party transfers to another Party in accordance with the provisions of Article 6 or Article 17 shall be subtracted from the assigned amount for the transferring party. . . . Any emission reduction units, or any part of any assigned amount, which a Party acquires from another Party in accordance with the provi-

---

3. For more detail, see *Environmental Markets* (Estrada-Oyeula 2000). A detailed analysis of the Kyoto Protocol can be found in *The Kyoto Protocol: A Guide and Assessment* (Grubb and Brack 1999).

sions of Article 6 or Article 17 shall be added to the assigned amount for the acquiring party" (Article 3, points 10 and 11). These are complex ways of saying that if I sell you some permits, then they count toward your allowed total and no longer count toward mine.

5. Joint implementation is allowed: "For the purposes of meeting its commitments under Article 3, any Party included in Annex I[4] may transfer to, or acquire from, any other such Party emission reduction units resulting from projects aimed at reducing anthropogenic emissions by sources or enhancing anthropogenic removal by sinks of greenhouse gases in any sector of the economy" (Article 6). This allows the United States to "buy" emission reductions by planting forests in another country: the United States could then have the carbon sequestration by these forests counted as a part of its emission reductions. It appears from the wording here that the other country should also be a member of Annex I, which is essentially the industrial countries plus the economies in transition, i.e., the former Soviet Union.

6. The Clean Development Mechanism (Article 12) appears to open up the possibility of joint implementation between industrial and developing countries. The relevant wording is "3(a) Parties not included in Annex I will benefit from project activities resulting in certified emission reductions; and (b) Parties included in Annex I may use the certified emission reductions accruing from such project activities to contribute to compliance with part of their quantified emission limitation and reduction commitments under Article 3."

The Kyoto Protocol and Forest Economics

To summarize the previous section, under the Kyoto Protocol, greenhouse gas emission targets are to be attained globally by issuing tradable carbon emission permits and operating the market exactly like the sulfur dioxide market in the United States. How does this agreement relate to the carbon sequestration role of forests? The key links

---

4. Annex I countries are defined in the Kyoto Protocol; essentially they are the industrialized countries.

are twofold. First, the market for tradable carbon emission permits puts a price on carbon sequestration. How? It sets the cost of abating carbon emissions, or of taking carbon out of the atmosphere. As the example above showed, businesses whose abatement costs exceed the price of a permit will buy permits rather than abate, and vice versa. So the price of a permit will set the cost of the most expensive abatement activity that will be used. In this sense the permit market puts a price on the abatement of carbon emissions. Any emission mechanism less expensive than the price of a permit makes economic sense, and no others do. So if we can sequester carbon in forests at a price less than or equal to the permit price, we have an option that would be attractive in economic terms.

The second link between markets for carbon emission permits and carbon sequestration in forests comes from the provisions of the Kyoto treaty. Two provisions are relevant. One allows industrial countries to engage in "joint implementation." This is a name for deals under which an industrial country pays another industrial country to reduce its emissions of greenhouse gases and then counts the reduction toward its own required reduction total under the protocol. Already there have been pilot schemes in which utility companies in the United States have paid for reforestation in Central America as a part of a joint implementation arrangement. In return for the payment they have received a credit for the amount of carbon sequestered.

The second provision that links tradable carbon emission permits to carbon sequestration in forests is called the "Clean Development Mechanism." The details of this mechanism were left imprecise at the 1997 Kyoto meeting. However, this mechanism is widely interpreted as admitting the possibility of paying countries, in particular both developing and industrial countries, for carbon sequestration. For the reasons set out above, the only reasonable rate for such payment would be the price of a carbon emission permit.

So, to summarize, the Kyoto Protocol of the Framework Convention on Climate Change could link the carbon sequestration role of forests to the market for tradable carbon emission permits. The extent to which this happens will depend on the final details of the Clean Development Mechanism, although the possibility of joint implementation seems assured as a part of the treaty's final version. So far it is clear that developing countries will be able to claim credits for carbon sequestration that occurs in the period 2008 to 2012 in forests established after 1990 on land not forested prior to 1990. The key point here is that indirectly the Kyoto Protocol will provide a market for one of the most valuable services of forests, the contribution that they make to the planetary carbon cycle—maintaining the balance of carbon dioxide, oxygen, and other gases in the atmosphere—and stabilizing the planet's climate. It has the potential to remedy what we have identified as a major shortcoming in the present global economic system, namely, its failure to translate the benefits of forest conservation into cash for those who conserve.

The Kyoto Protocol is not yet ratified. Assuming that eventually it is, what impact would this market for carbon sequestration services have? Assume also that the final version does allow countries to obtain credit for sequestering a ton of carbon in a forest at the then-current price for a permit to emit a ton of carbon. What will be the outcome?

It depends on two main factors. One is the price of a carbon emission permit: this will determine the market value of carbon sequestration. The other is the cost of sequestering carbon in forests. When the cost of sequestration is less than the market value of sequestration, the Kyoto Protocol will provide incentives for sequestration, and vice versa. The cost of sequestration will in turn depend on two factors. One is the amount of carbon that could be sequestered per unit of land: how much land must be used to sequester a ton of carbon? The other is the value of the land in alternative uses. This determines what landowners are giving up in order to sequester carbon. So, in summary, the amount of land needed to sequester a ton of carbon, together with the revenues that land could earn in other uses (such as cattle ranching or coffee growing) will fix the cost of sequestering carbon, which will have to be compared with the monetary rewards from sequestration.[5] Where the market value of sequestra-

---

5. It is possible that conserving a forest or reforesting will lead to an increase in revenues from watershed or ecotourism activities, which would offset some or all of the income lost from agriculture.

tion per hectare exceeds that of alternative uses (typically agricultural) per hectare, the land will probably be allotted to sequestration.

No one knows exactly what the value of tradable carbon emission permits will be when they are traded on a large scale.[6] Preliminary economic calculations[7] suggest that their value could be in the range of $15 to $100 per ton of carbon or equivalent. Such calculations are based on estimates of the supply of and demand for carbon emission permits under a Kyoto Protocol regime. Supply is taken to be the number of permits to be issued, already more or less agreed upon; the demand is based on current estimates of the cost of reducing carbon emissions. The range of emission-reduction technologies that may be adopted include switching from more to less carbon-intensive fuels—for example, from coal to natural gas. As noted earlier, the costs of these emission reduction technologies determine what people will be willing to pay for emission permits.

How much carbon can be sequestered per unit of land? Again there is a range of answers. In this case the uncertainty stems partly from ignorance and partly from the fact that there are many possible answers, depending on the soil, the climate, and the type of trees grown. The trees' age—where the forest is in its life cycle—is an important factor. Old trees take in less carbon than those in the middle of their growth period. When fully grown, trees sequester no net carbon: they both take it in via photosynthesis and emit it via respiration. Much of the carbon stored in a forest is in the soil rather than above ground, implying that even a detailed knowledge of tree types and ages is not sufficient to predict carbon storage. Allowing for all of these possibilities, sequestration rates are in the range of 0 to 15 tons per hectare (about 2.5 acres) per year, possibly more.[8] So

---

6. There is already a small market in carbon offsets on the Chicago Board of Trade. Costa Rica has been using this market.

7. The range of $10 to $50 emerges from simulations conducted by the Program on Information and Resources at Columbia University using a modified version of the OECD's GREEN computer model of the global economy. W. D. Nordhaus of Yale has reported estimates as high as $100 (personal communication).

8. Personal communication, Steve Pacala, Ecology Department, Princeton University.

sequestration of 1 ton might take as little as one-fifteenth of a hectare or a great deal more.

What could be earned from this land if it were kept in other uses? As in the earlier cases there is no precise number, only a number of points that determine a range. Ranching in Costa Rica can yield a maximum of about $120 net per hectare per year. By comparison, ranching in South Africa can generate about $25 per hectare per year and food crops about $70 per hectare per year (Anderson 1996). Numbers for other African countries seem lower. In Mexico the figures are comparable to those in Costa Rica: up to $100 to $150 per year as the net cash flow per hectare on the most efficient and modern farms and as little as a few dollars per hectare per year for subsistence farmers. Coffee plantations provide some exceptions at the high end, occasionally yielding as much as $200 per hectare per year. Banana plantations may return even more.[9]

In general it appears that if carbon sequestration can yield returns of $20 to $50 per hectare per year, it can be competitive with many of the uses of deforested land in many tropical countries. In other words, it could induce the replanting of forests that have been cut down. The land yielded by deforestation is usually unproductive, often on steep slopes vulnerable to erosion and flooding, so that the income lost by reforestation is not great and income from carbon sequestration would suffice to encourage reforestation if the return is in the lower part of the range mentioned above.

What do these numbers imply about the consequences of incentives for carbon sequestration? Carbon sequestration could produce income in the following range: if we take the lowest figures for the market price of carbon emission permits ($15 per ton) and a low figure for carbon sequestration rates (2 tons per hectare per year), we see that a hectare could earn $30 per year for carbon sequestration. At the upper ends of the ranges we have a carbon permit price of $100 and a sequestration rate of 15 tons per hectare per year, or $1,500 per hectare per year. In practice we might expect the earnings

---

9. Personal communication, Arturo Puente-Gonzales, National Institute for Forestry, Agriculture, and Livestock Research (INIFAP), Government of Mexico.

per hectare from sequestration to vary over the stage of the forest's life cycle, starting at zero, rising to $1,000 per year or more, and then dropping back to zero. The timing of this cycle would depend on the trees being grown, on soil and climate conditions, and on other variables. Reforesting would incur a one-time replanting cost for preparing land and buying and planting the seedlings, which might be as high as $900 per hectare.[10] Even with this initial cost, it seems possible that if the world as a whole pays for just one of the many services of tropical forests, then this could radically change the economics of forest conservation.

Open issues remain. For instance, what would be done with the forest when it reaches maturity? If the trees were tropical hardwood, they could be sold for timber that would most likely go to uses in which they would be preserved as timber—in furniture, houses, and so forth—and thus would not release the carbon previously sequestered. A fully mature forest no longer sequesters more carbon than it emits, and indeed, if it moves into a period of decay, it may actually become a net emitter of carbon. At this point the issue becomes prevention of the release of stored carbon rather than sequestration of additional carbon.

Conservation or Reforestation

How much land could be reforested under a system of this type? There is no solid evidence on this, but informed guesses suggest that it could be of the order of about 10 to 15 percent of all tropical forests. Perhaps even more important, what role would such a system play in preventing deforestation? Preventing deforestation is certainly greatly preferable to cutting down and then regrowing forests. It conserves carbon already sequestered in trees and soil and prevents the loss of biodiversity. In principle we should offer the same incentive for preserving forests that might be cut down as we do for reforesting already cut forestlands. Both have the same impact on the atmosphere. The problem here is a political one. If all carbon sequestration services were rewarded at the permit price, and not just those performed by new forests, then the amount of money to be paid to

---

10. Personal communication, Daniel Botkin, professor, Department of Biology, George Mason University.

tropical countries would probably exceed any number that the industrial countries, the main payers, would be willing to contribute. This is why the earlier citations from the Kyoto Protocol make no reference at all to maintaining forests intact, only to reforestation and deforestation. Any estimates of the amounts involved here are rough in the extreme, but existing tropical forests are estimated to cover about 2,727 million hectares (Reid 1998). Some of this may be mature and sequestering little additional carbon. Even if we take a low figure like $5 per hectare as the average value of sequestration services, we find a total annual payment for carbon sequestration to the tropical regions in the range of $13 billion annually. The total could be as high as $50 billion. As standards of comparison, the annual total of all overseas development assistance is currently about $60 billion, and in 1997 the total of private capital flows to the developing countries was about $90 billion. World population is about 6 billion, so the bill for carbon sequestration would be $2 to $10 per capita for everyone on Earth. For the population of industrial countries per capita, this comes to about $15 to $60 per year. In fact, many would probably feel that this is not a bad investment if it increases the chances of keeping the climate system intact and in addition maintains tropical forests and their biodiversity. Nevertheless, sums in excess of $13 billion are unlikely to be available for conservation of existing tropical forests under the Kyoto Protocol. This leaves the protocol in a form in which it can undo damage once it is done but not prevent it in the first place—not a satisfactory situation.

Costa Rica has suggested a compromise with respect to paying for sequestration through preservation of existing forests. Forest cover in Costa Rica, as in most tropical developing countries, has been declining for the last few decades. The government of Costa Rica has suggested that it should extrapolate its current and recent past rates of deforestation forward and use this as an estimate of what will happen to forest cover in the absence of active government intervention. The Costa Rican proposal is that this estimate should be used as the baseline from which to measure reforestation: any forest cover in excess of the estimate would count as reforestation. This method would enable a country to obtain some credit for forest conservation, thereby providing incentives for conservation while keeping the total sums paid to tropical countries for forest conservation to levels that are probably politically manageable. The downside is, of course, that there is an element of arbitrariness in determining the baseline above which we give credit for reforestation or for not deforesting. This might be a small price to pay for the resolution of so complex an issue.

In economic terms the discussion in this chapter demonstrates the following point: the sequestration of carbon by forests is a global public good, but it is typically difficult for the providers of such a service to appropriate all or even a significant part of the benefits, so that it is underprovided. A combination of a tradable permit system for greenhouse gas emissions plus issuing credits and incentives for sequestration may allow providers of sequestration services to capture the full economic value of what they provide.[11]

This could be an important step in closing the gap between the private and social returns of forestry. Currently the social returns for maintaining forest cover greatly exceed the private returns, with the obvious consequence that the amount of deforestation currently occurring is excessively large from an economic point of view.

The Kyoto Targets

As emphasized earlier, the permit trading mechanism of the Kyoto Protocol does not decide the target reductions in greenhouse gas emissions: that choice was made separately and was put at a reduction of 5 percent below 1990 levels by the period 2008–12. The target applies only to the so-called Annex I countries, which are mainly the industrial countries with the addition of the countries of the former Soviet Union. Developing countries are not included in Annex I. A reduction in the year 2008 to 5 percent below 1990 levels will probably amount to a reduction of about 30 percent below the emission levels that the Annex I countries would otherwise have reached by 2008.

This target level of emissions emerged from a complex process of bargaining and compromise at Kyoto and is not a level based on any

---

11. The assertion that markets give appropriate incentives for providing public goods is a surprising one to most economists in view of the free-rider problem. For a detailed analysis, see *Environmental Markets* (Chichilnisky and Heal 2000).

scientific or economic analysis. From an economic perspective, the appropriate emission targets are those at which the gains from an incremental tightening of the targets are just equal to the costs of tightening. The gains from a reduction in greenhouse gases are the avoided costs of further human-induced climate change, such as reduced agricultural output in developing countries, changes in the hydrological cycle, increases in the range of infectious-disease-carrying insects, and many more. The ideal abatement level is thus one at which these gains are just equal to the costs of a further reduction in greenhouse gases. Probably the target chosen in Kyoto is too low relative to what could really be justified by detailed analysis of the incremental costs and benefits from reducing greenhouse gas emissions: the gains from further tightening the emission standards beyond those agreed upon in Kyoto probably exceed the costs. However, the important point is certainly to start the process; details can be improved later.

The omission of developing countries from the Annex I category, those making commitments to reduce emissions under the protocol, is clearly a shortcoming. Large developing countries such as India and China may within decades be emitting as much in the way of greenhouse gases as the United States, a fact of which most participants are aware. The underlying problem is that the developing countries clearly feel that they need a substantial quid pro quo for giving up the right to industrialize by following the fossil-fuel route followed by the now-industrialized countries. Furthermore, they feel that the current greenhouse gas problem is the responsibility of the industrial countries, whose consumption of fossil fuels has created it. It follows, in the opinion of many developing countries, that the industrial countries should shoulder the burden for correcting the present problem. It is possible that payment for some of the ecosystem services provided by the natural assets of developing countries could be a big part of the solution.

Payments for carbon sequestration on the scale mentioned above would be a substantial inducement for their agreement with the protocol, particularly if combined with a distribution of emission permits that favors the developing countries. The establishment of property rights in the atmosphere creates wealth for those to whom they are distributed, so a fraction of that wealth could be an attractive bargaining counter. Chapter 2 noted that the Coasian resolution of external effects can be accomplished in several ways, which have quite different implications for the distribution of wealth. In Coase's example of a factory polluting a community, we can give the polluter the right to pollute or we can give the local community the right to clean air. Either establishes property rights and so can lead to an efficient outcome. But in the first case the polluter is enriched by the newly created property rights, and in the second case the community benefits in this way.

A similar issue arises in the context of the Kyoto Protocol. Greenhouse gases are the source of an excess of social-over-private costs, an externality. To remedy this, the rights to emit greenhouse gases can be given to the existing polluters, the industrial countries. Alternatively, they can be given to developing countries or some combination of both. In the former case the developing countries will have to buy permits from industrial countries, and in the latter the reverse is true: the industrial countries will have to purchase permits from developing countries. The sums involved could amount to hundreds of billions of U.S. dollars, so the difference matters. Giving permits to the existing polluters is known as "grandfathering"; the opposing model is that permits would be distributed on a per capita basis, on the grounds that all citizens of the Earth have an equal right to use the atmosphere. In this case most permits would go to developing countries. There is a potential here for providing a significant monetary incentive for the developing countries to join the Kyoto Protocol.

In summary, in spite of several shortcomings, the Kyoto Protocol is undoubtedly a real step forward. It does make a constructive attempt to grasp the problem of climate change, and it can set an important precedent by establishing a monetary value for some aspects of ecosystem services.

Chapter 6

Biodiversity

Biodiversity is difficult to define. It is likewise difficult to succinctly describe its role in supporting human activities, but its importance is nonetheless real.

Biodiversity is short for "biological diversity," a term biologists use to denote the total variety of biological entities and the variability among them. This variability occurs at many levels. There is biological variability between different species at the level of the community or collection of species, between different members of species, and between different members of a population (a geographically distinct group of members of a given species). There is no single or simple measure of biodiversity: none of the attempts to construct one has been generally accepted.

Variability within a species is a familiar concept: your genes are different from mine, yet both of us are members of the species *Homo sapiens*. So within a species there is a gene pool, with genetic variation within that pool. Animal and plant breeders use this variation when trying to breed for particular characteristics: they find members of the species with the characteristics they seek and interbreed them. This is called *selective breeding*. In economic terms, genetic variation is a resource: it provides a pool of within-species differences on which we can draw when seeking to develop new varieties of species.

Plant breeders find another use for genetic diversity within a species, by developing varieties resistant to disease. Different varieties of the same species have different degrees of susceptibility to any particular disease. If one were to plant a single variety and a disease to which it is susceptible were to strike, the entire planting would be destroyed. If instead one plants different varieties, which will typically differ in their susceptibility to a disease, then there is some insurance against complete crop loss. The Irish potato famine of the nineteenth century is an example of the extreme hardship caused by growing a single variety of potato, *Solanum tuberosum*. So genetic variation at the species level is economically valuable and has historically been the source of almost all agricultural progress.

Why is biodiversity economically important?[1] We can classify the reasons under four headings:

- Productivity
- Insurance
- Knowledge
- Provision of ecosystem services

Although there is some overlap among them, these categories provide a helpful guide for thinking through the significance of biodiversity from the perspective of economics. We have already touched on the second and third categories: genetic variability provides insurance against total losses from disease, and it helps us develop new varieties, thereby providing knowledge. Let's look at these four roles in more depth.

Biodiversity and Productivity

How does biodiversity contribute to productivity? Experimental evidence suggests that for some plant communities, those with more biodiversity are on average more productive than those with less. Tilman (Tilman and Downing 1994) planted similar plots of land

---

1. I am focusing here exclusively on the economic reasons that biodiversity is important to human beings. There are many other reasons one might wish to preserve biodiversity. In particular, one might feel a moral imperative not to be responsible for destroying other forms of life.

with different varieties of grassland plants, some with a large number of species, some with much fewer. Each plot was planted with the same mix year after year, and several indicators of plot performance were recorded. These included the proportion of available nutrients that were taken up by the plants—a measure of the community's efficiency in using resources—and the amount of biomass grown. *Biomass* refers to the total dry weight of the plants: it is a measure of the growing that they do. We can also define it as the amount of carbon from the atmosphere that is photosynthesized into carbohydrate. Tilman found over about twenty years that on average the more diverse plots performed better than the less diverse ones.

What does "more diverse" or "less diverse" mean here? There are two dimensions to diversity. The first is diversity of functional groups, or of plant types. The second is diversity of plant species within a functional group. So "more diverse" means having either more functional groups or more plant types within each functional group, or both, represented. Plants are classified into functional groups on the basis of their intrinsic physiological and morphological characteristics, such as whether they fix nitrogen, have three or four carbon photosynthetic pathways, are woody, are annuals or perennials, grow in early spring or late summer, and so forth. Beans and other legumes that fix nitrogen—nitrogen fixers—are one functional group. Woody plants—plants that have aboveground tissue that survives from one year to another—are another group. Two other important groups are C-3 and C-4 grasses: the postscripts 3 and 4 denote the numbers of carbon atoms in their photosynthetic pathways. C-3 grasses grow best in the cool seasons—spring and fall—whereas C-4 grasses are warm-season grasses. Forbs—broadleaved plants that do not fix nitrogen—are another functional group (Tilman, Naeem, et al. 1997). These different types represent unique solutions to life's constraints and tradeoffs. For example, perennials invest heavily in durable infrastructure that survives from year to year while annuals invest each year in a completely new structure. Such characteristics influence water and nutrient requirements, the pattern of growth over the seasons, and life history.

One key aspect of diversity is measured by the number of different functional groups represented by the plants in a given area. This is called, not surprisingly, *functional diversity.* In this sense a group of four plants from four functional groups is more diverse than a group of ten from one or two groups. A group consisting of a legume, a woody plant, and a forb is more functionally diverse than six different grasses.

Species diversity refers to the number of different species within each functional group, or the total number of species present. This latter measure is sometimes called *diversity per se.* Clearly there is a correlation between diversity per se, the total number of different species present, and functional diversity. One cannot add more species without eventually adding more functional groups as well, as there is only a limited number of species in each functional group. Another related determinant of productivity is the composition of the functional groups present: productivity may depend not just on the number of such groups represented but also on their identities, as some groups may be more important than others in contributing to productivity or the ability to survive environmental fluctuations.

Tilman's study showed that the average amount of biomass grown per year on a plot of a given size increased with the diversity of functional groups represented, as shown in Figure 6.1. The increase leveled off after a certain point, above which more diversity added little to the community's performance. Tilman and co-workers also found more nutrient uptake and better soil quality on plots with

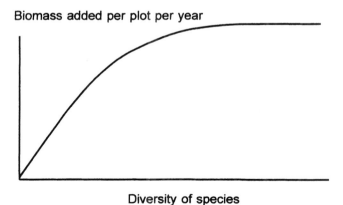

FIGURE 6.1. The productivity of a plant community may increase with species diversity.

a more diverse collection of plant species. Furthermore, the plots that were more diverse in this sense were also more robust in the face of weather fluctuations. It appears from this work that both functional diversity and species diversity are important in maintaining productivity and resilience.

What is the mechanism behind these results? There is still some dispute. One possibility is that each plant type is best suited to a particular range of weather conditions. Weather varies from year to year in terms of temperature, rainfall, and many other aspects. If an area contains only one plant type, in many years there will be no plants well adapted to the weather in those years. If, however, many types grow in an area, then in most years some will be well adapted and on average productivity will be greater. It is another illustration of the old proverb "Don't put all your eggs in one basket." Analytically, it illustrates the same point as the economic argument for holding a diversified portfolio of stocks: the more diversified your portfolio, the less vulnerable you are to conditions that are bad for particular stocks or stocks in a particular sector of the economy. A robust portfolio should contain different types of stocks: stocks that do well in times of growth, stocks that do well in times of high-interest rates, and stocks that do relatively well in times of recession. Areas with diverse growth will also be more resilient to weather variation, as a part of the same phenomenon. This is related to the insurance role of biological diversity, here manifested as higher average productivity.

There are additional mechanisms through which this relationship between diversity and productivity may operate. Many plants live in a symbiotic relationship with fungi that are associated with their root systems. These fungi play a crucial role in allowing the plants to take up nutrients essential to their growth, especially nitrogen. An alternative explanation (suggested by Read 1998 and Van der Heijden, Klironomos, et al. 1998) for the greater productivity of mixed plant communities is based on the interactions between these fungal communities in the soil, which increase the effectiveness of nutrient uptake. Similar studies have been conducted for microbial communities and have found similar results. Again they show that more diverse communities are on average more stable and robust in the face of environmental fluctuations. (For reviews of this area, see

Grime 1997; Hooper and Vitousek 1997; McGrady-Steed, Harris, et al. 1997; and Naeem and Li 1997.)

There are other arguments about why diversity raises productivity, mostly specific to particular biological communities. Forests provide a good example. Some trees are tolerant of shade and others of bright light. A forest of a uniform tree species will consist entirely of trees of one of these types. In contrast, in a multispecies forest tall shade-intolerant trees will form the upper canopy, below them shorter, more shade-tolerant trees, and perhaps below them another layer of even more shade-tolerant trees or shrubs. With such an arrangement of diverse species, bright light falls on those that most need it, and the less intense light that passes through their canopy then falls on plants well suited to it. Total photosynthesis—that is, conversion of carbon dioxide in the air to carbohydrates with the aid of light energy—will be greater than in a single-species forest because of the more efficient use of light energy from the sun (Aber and Melillo 1991).

These arguments indicate that diversity is important in ensuring the productivity and robustness of natural ecosystems, and therefore of the Earth's life-support systems, which depend on and indeed are composed of these natural ecosystems. Diversity helps natural ecosystems make the best adjustments to changes in environmental conditions. Without the appropriate level of diversity, natural ecosystems cannot adjust to natural variations in the environment. On this topic, an interesting article by Chapin, Walker, et al. (1997) concludes that

> genetic and species diversity per se are important to long-term maintenance of community and ecosystem structure and processes. This argues that no two species are ecologically redundant, even if they appear similar in their ecosystem effects under one particular set of environmental conditions.

The productivity of agricultural systems depends on rich sources of genetic material and therefore provides an extremely pragmatic justification for conserving biodiversity. The great increases in grain yields of the "green revolution" of the 1960s and 1970s, which were responsible for keeping food output growing in parallel with population in developing countries, were largely achieved through development of new plant varieties. There are estimates suggesting that as much as $1 billion has been added to the value of U.S. agricultural output each year for the last half-century as a result of plant breeders' use of genetic diversity. Specifically, in the last half-century we have seen a doubling in yields of rice, barley, soybeans, wheat, cotton, and sugar cane; a threefold increase in tomato yields; and a quadrupling in yields of maize, sorghum, and potato (National Research Council 1999). All of this has been based on and derived from genetic variability in the underlying plant populations. Plant breeders improve a crop by finding a variety that has a desired characteristic—drought tolerance, for example—and then crossing it with commercial varieties. Some of the offspring of the cross will usually show both the target characteristic—drought tolerance in this case—and the high yields typical of the commercial variety. In economic terms, this variability is an asset, and one that has yielded great return at little cost.

The practice of crop rotation is an application of the biodiversity concept that contributes to agricultural productivity. Changing from one crop to another from one year to the next can increase soil nutrients and enhance its productivity. For example, rotating a crop such as wheat with a legume that fixes nitrogen can prevent long-term nitrogen loss and reduce the need for nitrogen fertilizers. This type of crop rotation was characteristic of traditional agricultural practices in medieval Europe.

Biodiversity serves agriculture by means of other essential services, such as pollination and pest control. Many agricultural crops require pollination, which depends on the presence of insects (often bees) and birds. It is well documented that bird and insect species often provide the most reliable and cost-effective method of pest control. But environmental changes and pesticide use threaten these species and reduce yields of some crops (Nabhan and Buchmann 1996; Nabhan and Buchmann 1997).

It is important to note that while biodiversity contributes to the productivity of both natural ecosystems and agricultural systems, it does so through different mechanisms. Natural systems benefit directly from a diverse mix of species; agricultural systems benefit from the existence of a pool of genetic variability on which breeders can draw. Agricultural systems are usually monocultures—that is, a single species is grown intensively over a large area. Its growth is supported by applications of water, fertilizers, pesticides, and weedkillers. Farmers manage cropland so as to ensure that crop growth is not limited by lack of water or nutrients, and that the main food crop is not damaged by pests or does not have to compete with other species. Farmers create and maintain an artificial environment, planting crops that are optimally adjusted to this environment, an approach that is radically different from the natural growth process.

Biodiversity and Insurance

Chapter 1 described the use of a previously noncommercial variety of rice in the development of a form resistant to the grassy stunt virus, thereby preventing heavy crop losses. Similar stories have occurred with other food crops, in particular corn in the United States (Myers 1997). We have every reason to expect that events like these will recur regularly: planting large areas with genetically identical plants greatly increases the chances that once a disease starts, it will spread with dangerous speed through the entire area and crop.

Such cases illustrate clearly that biodiversity is an important protection against disastrous new diseases. The pathogens that cause disease are evolving continually in an attempt to outwit our defenses against them. Our defenses then evolve in response, an example of what biologists call *coevolution* (Ehrlich and Raven 1964).

An apt example of this phenomenon is the evolution of antibiotic resistance among bacteria. The bacteria that cause several once-common diseases in humans are now showing resistance to their principal controls, to the great concern of public-health authorities (Morell 1997; Witte 1998). The same is happening with the pathogens that cause crop and livestock diseases. The problem is rendered particularly acute by the short generation time of bacteria and other pathogens and by the rapidity with which genetic material can be transferred between organisms. It is precisely the genetic variability of pathogens that allows them to develop resistance to antibiotics and our other defenses against them—that is, some of the disease-causing pathogens are naturally relatively unaffected by our defenses against them, which may be in the form of weedkillers, insecticides, or serums. These more resistant specimens are the ones that survive and from which new subsequent generations are bred. Without diversity to draw from, we are disarmed unilaterally in the war against our most threatening enemies.

There is another important role for the insurance provided by biodiversity: to provide the genetic variability needed to adapt to environmental change. We are making changes to the global environment on an unprecedented scale, and biodiversity may be critical in allowing us to respond to them. A hotter climate may require different crop varieties. A rise in sea level may lead to increased salinity in groundwater and thus to a need for salt-tolerant crop varieties. Geographical diversity—different varieties of the same species that grow in many different regions with different temperature ranges and different soil conditions—may assist us in adapting to new conditions and support populations.

Biodiversity and Genetic Knowledge

Biodiversity's store of genetic material is a priceless source of knowledge. A good example is provided by the polymerase chain reaction (PCR), a reaction central to the amplification of DNA specimens for analysis, as in forensic tests used in criminal investigations and many processes central to the biotechnology industry. Culturing—the process of taking a minute sample of DNA and multiplying it manyfold—requires an enzyme that is resistant to high temperatures. Enzymes with the right degree of temperature resistance were found in organisms in the hot springs in Yellowstone National Park and used to develop an enzyme for culturing DNA specimens. This enzyme is now central to the rapidly growing biotechnology industry.

There are many more less-complex examples. In fact, 37 percent of the value of the pharmaceuticals sold in the United States are or were originally derived from plants or other living organisms (Carte 1996). Aspirin comes from the bark of willow trees. A drug effective against ovarian cancer is derived from the bark of yew trees. A derivative of the rosy periwinkle flower (Catharanthus roseus, also called Madagascar periwinkle) is being used to cure childhood leukemia.

Certain plants and animals produce substances that are highly active pharmacologically. For example, some snakes produce venom that paralyzes parts of the nervous system; venom from some other species reduces blood pressure. Some insects produce anticoagulants. All of these have been adapted for medical use. There is little that is new in these observations: they form the basis for many traditional medicines, which rely almost exclusively on plants. We have all heard the commonly expressed argument for preserving the Amazon Basin: it contains heretofore-undiscovered plants and animals that may offer cures for disease in the future.

Biodiversity and Ecosystem Services

We have already seen that genetic diversity provides raw material for selective breeding, the traditional way of developing new crop or animal varieties that are more productive, more disease-resistant, hardier, or more desirable in some other way. We have also looked at its role in ensuring the productivity of ecosystems and in ensuring their robustness against diseases and pathogens. There are other, more complex ways in which biodiversity is essential to the proper functioning of ecosystems and to the delivery of the ecosystem services upon which human beings are so dependent. Indeed, one can only speculate on the extent of this complexity. On the one hand, there are cases in which an ecosystem's full diversity of organisms is required for that system to function and to provide services to human societies. On the other hand, the removal (or addition) of even a single type of organism can have extraordinarily far-reaching consequences. Ecologists have used the term *keystone species* to describe a species whose removal will cause an entire ecosystem to change substantially.

A widely cited example of a keystone species is that of sea otters on the California coast. The hunting of sea otters for their pelts led to extensive and undesirable changes in California coastal ecosystems. Sea otters eat sea urchins, which in turn graze on kelp plants. Without control of the urchin population by otters, the urchins destroy the kelp beds, leading to a greatly impoverished coastal environment. A ban on otter hunting contributed to the ecosystem's restoration to its original state.

Another example of the role and impact of a keystone species is provided by the removal of kangaroo rats from an area of the Chihuahuan Desert, which resulted in a threefold increase in the yields of grasses and to far-reaching changes in the desert ecosystem. In this case the rats had played a key role in hindering plant growth, eating seeds and disturbing the soil surface. Their removal allowed native plant species to propagate (see Power, Tilman, et al. 1996 and Baskin 1997).

Not only can the removal of a species lead to big changes in an ecosystem; the introduction of a new species (a so-called exotic species) can cause a profound transformation. A dramatic example is the 1890 introduction of the rinderpest virus, which attacks domestic and wild cattle, into East Africa. By 1892, 95 percent of the wildebeest in the Serengeti region had died, together with most of the domestic cattle. Wildebeest are one of the main grazers and also the main food sources for carnivorous predators (lions, leopards, hyenas) in the Serengeti, so their virtual elimination led to profound changes in the system. In the 1930s the introduction of a vaccination against rinderpest reestablished the original system (Aber and Melillo 1991; Sinclair 1979).

The point of these examples is that we cannot easily tell a priori which species are essential and which are not. There is often a risk that an apparently small change in a set of species will have effects far beyond those initially anticipated. The degree of interdependence between different species is great, so that human well-being may depend on many more species than we would expect from a first analysis of the situation. Abelard, an eleventh-century French theologian, suggested that any organism has a role to play and a reason for existing: "Whatever is generated is generated by some necessary cause, for nothing comes into being except there be some due cause for it" (quoted in National Research Council 1999).

There is another aspect of the contribution of biodiversity to ecosystem functioning. A particular role in an ecosystem may be played at different times or under different circumstances by quite different plants or animals. The type of tree that stabilizes soil on a north-facing slope at a certain latitude may not grow on a south-facing slope at that latitude, so that a different species is needed there to maintain the physical stability of the slope. In other words, the set of species required for a certain type of ecosystem to function may vary greatly from region to region. In fact, we know of no single subset of species that on its own would serve to operate all ecosystems and provide all ecosystem services in all regions of the planet. So diversity in a given location may increase productivity and ecosystem functions in that location, while diversity at the regional or global level is actually necessary for the operation of important ecosystems in all geographic regions. While individual species may possibly be redundant in some locations, it is possible that at the global scale few, if any, are. (For more on the role of biodiversity in maintaining the supply of ecosystem services, see Daily and Dasgupta 2000.)

Biodiversity and Markets

To return to economic issues, to what extent is there scope for commercializing these contributions of biodiversity? Obviously they are economically important, but can the market capture them? Recall that we have classified the contributions of biodiversity under four headings: increasing productivity, and providing insurance, knowledge, and ecosystem services. The following sections look at each in turn.

Productivity

Farmers achieve some of the benefits of diversity through crop rotation, planting different crops in successive years. The use of varied crop types makes different demands on the soil and contributes different nutrients to it. However, the range of crops used for this purpose is quite limited and does not contribute in any substantial way to the conservation of biodiversity.

Another mechanism through which diversity promotes agricultural productivity is via its contribution to the development of new plant species that are better adapted to emerging conditions or more resistant to new diseases. At this point the productivity and knowledge roles of biodiversity merge.

There appears to be some appreciation of the benefits of diversity in tropical agriculture, where there is a tendency to grow several crops together or to grow crops in a way that conserves the original forest. Traditionally coffee, a shade-tolerant plant, was grown as an understory plant beneath high tropical forest trees. This practice means that canopy trees need not be destroyed to make land available for coffee growing and allows other commercial crops, such as citrus fruits and avocados, to be grown as well, so farmers can diversify their risks. Moreover, it contributes to the preservation of diversity because the forest is conserved. Studies have shown that forests converted for production of shade-grown coffee retain a very large proportion of their original biodiversity, and that this type of production is less expensive per pound than plantation growing. This cost difference reflects in part the greater productivity of diverse ecosystems and the more effective cycling of nutrients in these plant communities. (The total yield of coffee per hectare is, however, less [Perfecto, Rice, et al. 1996]). In this case, it seems that the productivity enhancements of diverse systems can be realized commercially, with attendant benefits for biodiversity conservation.

Insurance

Insurance is clearly something for which there is a demand. People purchase all manner of insurance to protect against loss. So perhaps the insurance role of biodiversity is one for which people will pay. The difficulty here is that until recently this insurance has been provided as a public good—indeed, as a global public good.

Consider the example described in Chapter 1, the International Rice Research Institute's development of a rice variety resistant to damage by the grassy stunt virus. In this case, the protection afforded by the newly developed variety was provided as a public good. It was available to all for the usual cost of seed rice. The developers could not exclude from its use those who did not contribute to its development by paying insurance premiums.

Could the problem be overcome by charging a premium price for the new variety? This would not resolve the issue either, as this price would be paid only after the product had been developed and consumers identified a need for it. If the new variety were never needed, then this price premium would never be paid. An insurance premium, however, is paid whether the insurance will be needed or not. The nature of an insurance contract is that I pay for insurance now, before I know whether I need it. The same is true of all risk-sharing arrangements. In a framework in which the insurance offered by bio-diversity is a public good, as we saw in Chapter 2, the incentives to retain and develop biodiversity for its insurance role are inadequate from an economic perspective.

This possibly will change. Public goods can become private goods, through either institutional or technical change. A good example is television broadcasting. Until about ten years ago, this was a public good par excellence: it was nonexcludable, because a broadcaster could not exclude anyone in the reception area from viewing a program, and of course there is no rivalry in consumption, because my viewing of a TV broadcast in no way interferes with yours. The development of scramblers changed this. A TV broadcast can now be scrambled so that it can be viewed only by those who have purchased a descrambler. Broadcasters can now exclude those who have not paid from viewing their programs, which are therefore no longer public goods. A public good has been privatized.

Developments in the area of intellectual property rights for agri-cultural biotechnology could change the situation in a similar way for the insurance value of biodiversity, leading to the privatization of a hitherto-public good. Crop developers are increasingly patenting genes developed to enhance the properties of crops, including such aspects as their taste, productivity, and insect resistance. Most agri-cultural biotechnology companies have a large and growing portfolio of patents on genes and on genetically modified plant varieties. They are also aggressively defending these patents, to the extent of devel-oping and introducing "terminator genes" that will ensure that the offspring of these plants are sterile, although Monsanto has recently agreed that these will not be deployed without further research into their impacts. It is possible that plant breeders with such a tight hold on their intellectual property will be able to extract from users a great enough return to justify substantial investment in biodiversity conser-vation. The aggressive enforcement of intellectual property rights might act here like scramblers did with TV broadcasts, effectively pri-vatizing a previously public good. Were it to happen, this would increase substantially the incentives for biodiversity conservation, but possibly at the cost of restricting access to the latest agricultural tech-nology to those with the ability to pay a premium.

There is already a good illustration of the complex possible side effects of privatizing genetic knowledge. The bacterium *Bacillus thuringiensis* (BT) is a natural pesticide that controls many crop pests. For this reason organic farmers have used it as a pesticide; being biodegradable, it leaves no dangerous residues on the crops on which it is used. Monsanto recently incorporated genes from BT into genetically modified crops. The presence of these genes in the plants means that the plant itself benefits from the defense used by the BT bacteria, which is the production of proteins that are toxic to the main pests of cotton and corn. Because BT is now being used widely, it is probable that pests will develop resistance to it. Resistance to a defense evolves faster the more extensively it is used, so within a few years we can expect generations of immune crop pests. Monsanto will seek to develop variants on the BT genes, and given its scientific and financial resources, will probably succeed. It will sell a new generation of transgenic plants with defenses against the new generation of pests. However, these will be Monsanto's proprietary products covered by its patents. Organic farmers will no longer be able to use BT or its derivatives as a harmless pesticide because of the evolution of resistant pathogen strains. This is a clear illustration of the two factors mentioned above: development of intellectual property rights in genetic knowledge leading to both stronger incentives to conserve and to develop further, and to a restriction of access. In the case of transgenic crops including BT defenses, Monsanto recently announced that all growers of BT corn will be required to grow plots of nonengineered corn that are at least 20 percent the size of the engineered crops. The aim here is to provide sufficient nonengineered corn so that the development of resistant pests will be delayed or possibly even prevented (*Nature* 1999).

Knowledge

Let's now look at the role of biodiversity as a source of knowledge. There are two different areas of application here: the development of medical products by the pharmaceutical industry, and the development of new or better crops by the agricultural biotechnology industry.

In applications of biodiversity to the development of pharmaceuticals there has already been some progress toward commercialization. Recognition of the likelihood that tropical plants contain chemicals that could be forerunners of pharmaceuticals has led most major drug companies to pursue bioprospecting as a way of finding new pharmacologically active substances to serve as a basis for drug development. Typically they have sought these compounds in the tropics, in areas where there is extensive interspecies competition. They have been willing to pay quite substantial sums for access to these regions and have made deals with host countries that give them royalties on the resulting products. Such royalties could be large relative to the incomes of the countries concerned.

For example, Merck, one of the largest pharmaceutical companies in the United States, has an agreement with a Costa Rican agency called InBio (Instituto Nacional de la Biodiversidad) for bioprospecting rights in Costa Rica. The terms of the agreement are that Merck paid InBio a fixed sum, $1.35 million, to be used for forest conservation, in exchange for the right to receive samples collected by InBio and to use these as the basis for new product development. Should any of them prove commercially successful, Merck will pay InBio a royalty on the revenues generated. Similar agreements are in place between other U.S. pharmaceutical companies and regions of Central and South America.

In another case, Shaman Pharmaceuticals, a startup biotechnology company in California, is using ethnobotanical research as its main avenue for drug prospecting. It is building on the fact that traditional healers in many societies use extracts from plants and insects or reptiles for treating diseases and is following the leads that emerge from this body of traditional knowledge. Hence the company's name: a shaman is a medicine man or healer. Shaman has agreed to share its profits with the societies from which it derives its successful leads.

Other such agreements are being struck. In 1999 the pharmaceutical multinational Glaxo Wellcome and a small Brazilian biotechnology company signed a $3.2 million contract to screen up to 30,000 compounds of plant, fungal, and bacterial origin from several regions in Brazil. As part of the three-year deal, the companies agreed that one-quarter of any royalties arising from successfully exploited patents will be used to support community-based conservation, health, and education projects. Another 25 percent of the royalties will go to the university group responsible for isolating and identifying the product. Glaxo Wellcome will pay for all research and development costs in Brazil. The research will focus on compounds found in the Amazonian and Atlantic rainforests, and Glaxo Wellcome will have an option to license any product arising from it (Bonalume and Dickson 1999).

The discovery of the PCR enzyme, the agreement between Merck and InBio, and several other drug discoveries based on plants from developing countries have led to a wave of optimism, some perhaps excessive, about the potential commercial value of in situ biodiversity in developing countries.

What in fact is the commercial potential here? There is no question that pharmaceutical and agricultural products of great human and commercial value have been and will be developed from the biodiversity in tropical countries. The key question is how much of this value will be returned as a reward for the conservation of the originating biodiversity. In answering this question, we have to take note of several points. One is that an immense amount of human skill and expertise is needed to go from a plant specimen to a commercial drug. Typically there will be a minimum of ten or more years of work by hundreds of skilled people working with millions of dollars of sophisticated equipment. A second point is that very few plant extracts—probably less than 1 in 10,000—actually produce drug leads—that is, pharmacologically active compounds with no obvious ill effects. Of these, very few become commercial drugs, again less than 1 in 100. On average, perhaps 1 in 250,000 samples leads to a commercial drug (*Nature* 1998).

The picture that emerges, then, is that the chance of any individual bioprospecting operation leading to a commercially valuable drug is very small indeed. And even if it does produce a drug, tens or even hundreds of millions of dollars will have to be invested, with significant chances of failure right to the end.

Nevertheless, developments in biotechnology are altering these prospects. They are reducing the time needed for testing and development and providing greater insights into the kinds of chemicals likely to be successful. By reducing the costs of drug development based on bioprospecting, they are making bioprospecting more attractive. To give some precision to this effect, ten years ago the cost of screening 10,000 samples for pharmaceutical potential would have been $6 million; today it is $150,000 (Reid, Laird, et al. 1993). At the same time, advances in knowledge, based on understanding of the cellular and genetic mechanisms of disease, are making alternative methods of drug development more effective. In total, the picture that emerges here is one of heavily guarded optimism. Bioprospecting does have economic value, and technological developments may be increasing that value. However, in the short term we cannot expect great sums of money to flow to the conservation of biological diversity from bioprospecting possibilities.

Real data on the significance of bioprospecting will emerge only slowly, as the development and testing of drugs is slow—in at least ten years. However, recent calculations have suggested that in a small number of the world's biodiversity hotspots, bioprospecting rights may be worth as much as $9,000 per hectare (about 2.5 acres). This is small in relation to the amount that might ultimately be derived from drug sales, but large relative to other uses of the land. In fact, it is about a century of ranching income (Rausser and Small 2000). The key insight to be derived from these calculations is that prior knowledge of the nature of the ecosystems in a location can improve estimates of the probability of finding commercially interesting compounds there and can suggest where research would be profitable and where success would be unlikely. Indeed, it can change the odds of success from 1 in 10,000 to something an order of magnitude better. In practical terms, developing countries can identify the commercial attractions of their biodiversity by research on the ecosystems of which it is a part. This is rather like a country with potential oil reserves engaging in basic geological prospecting before seeking to negotiate leases for oil development. The results may be positive or negative, but either way they will provide a better view of its prospects. In those cases in which the research is positive, the impact on the value of prospecting rights could be large.

There is a further problem to be overcome in establishing an income flow from bioprospecting—a problem involving intellectual property rights. The same plant may occur in several different regions, and the same or similar chemicals may occur in different plants. So the same or similar drugs may be derived by different routes from different plants or different geographic regions. Research toward a commercial product has to be well under way before it is patentable, so that there is always a risk that a new product will be blocked by a prior patent. There is also a risk, as far as the conservation of biodiversity is concerned, that biodiversity is valuable but leads to no direct commercial application. A recent article on the value of marine bioprospecting (Carte 1996) made this point very clearly:

> Although many of these products are not likely to become therapeutics, the information gained from studying them is likely to lead to the development and understanding of novel molecular targets, which may in turn lead to the development of new therapeutic agents.

This is a classic statement of the value of basic knowledge—its importance is great, but it's not patentable and not something that can be appropriated by a typical bioprospecting contract with a royalty payment or revenue sharing. We need more constructive thinking about how to realize the undoubted importance of bioprospecting in terms of income for conservation.

A further illustration of this point is provided by the example of taxol. Taxol is a promising antitumor agent in breast and ovarian cancers that can be extracted from a fungus that lives in the phloem (inner bark) of the Pacific yew. Taxol was first isolated from the tree itself, but the tree is relatively rare and slow-growing and produces little taxol, so a search for other sources was initiated (Stierle, Stroble, et al. 1993). Ultimately, little in the way of economic returns may flow to the regions in which taxol was discovered.

Biodiversity can also be applied to the development of new or better crops. To date this has probably been the most important commercial application of biodiversity. As noted several times, the existence of a pool of genetic variation provides plant and animal breeders with the raw materials for developing new varieties and more productive or resilient variants of existing varieties. The existing varieties of a commercially important crop are by now usually the property of a commercial firm or research facility and are protected by patents. As an example, the University of California owns the patents of many strawberry varieties—varieties that are best suited to different soil types and different weather conditions, that are least prone to spoiling during transport and storage, and so on. For almost all other commercial crops, the varieties are owned by seed companies, whose main asset is often the intellectual property represented by their ownership of patents to widely used varieties. In this context, the market can certainly recognize the value of biodiversity, provided that it is of the type that seems likely to contribute to the development and refinement of commercially important crops. Unusual variants of commercial crops, such as early variants of wheat, corn, or soybeans, would qualify; so possibly would their near genetic relatives. But biodiversity more broadly would probably not derive a value through this process, even though genes from unrelated plants might enhance the commercial potential of existing crops.

Ecosystem Services

Most of the services provided by natural ecosystems are dependent on adequate and appropriate biodiversity. So in selling any of these services we are obtaining an economic return on biodiversity. The previous three chapters have given some indication of the potential for sales of ecosystem services to generate important incentives and have suggested that in the cases of watershed services, ecotourism, and carbon sequestration there is real potential, some of which is already being realized.

There are other economic mechanisms through which some tropical forests might be conserved, though it is not clear how generalized they can become. One is the sale of what are called "nontimber forest products." These are commercially valuable forest products that are not produced by tree cutting. They are therefore not timber, and their limited harvest and sale is compatible with forest conservation. They include various tropical fruits, vines that can be used as ropes, rattan (which grows among trees), resins such as latex, and plants used as medicine by local populations. This last use is important: about 4 billion people have no access to Western-style medicine and depend for treatment in times of sickness on plant extracts. This is a market that is important in human terms; the amounts of money involved are small by comparison with those in Western medicine but could still be enough to provide a significant incentive. Recent estimates suggest that in some tropical forests the collection and sale of nontimber forest products could yield as much as $60 to $140 per hectare per year, although there is controversy about the generality of such numbers (Grimes, Loomis, et al. 1994). As we have noted in earlier discussions of ranching and carbon sequestration, these are significant numbers. Given that these numbers are sustainable—i.e., can be earned year after year—they are probably sufficient to justify conservation of forests even in the face of pressure for logging. However, at the moment we have a limited number of studies of this form of forest use, so that it is not clear how generally applicable these numbers are.

These different mechanisms for generating income from natural systems are not mutually exclusive: the same land area could earn income by all five mechanisms. A forest could obtain returns from carbon sequestration, bioprospecting, nontimber products, watershed management, and ecotourism. In fact, the region of the Mata Atlantica (a Brazilian coastal rainforest) inland from Rio de Janeiro is in a position to do exactly this. It manages the watershed for Rio in much the way that the Catskills region does for New York. It also manages the stream flow of the Rio Paraibo do Sul, which provides most of the electric power for Rio via hydropower. These two services make it truly a major utility for Rio with great economic value. Additionally, it supports a wide range of endemic species, sequesters carbon, and is a magnet for tourists. Currently the region obtains a financial return on only one of these activities, ecotourism. In a case such as this, it is clear that the economic incentives for conservation could be immense if we were only to do effectively what we already know how to do.[2]

---

2. All of these measures are consistent with the United Nations Convention on Biological Diversity, to which many nations (though not the United States at the time of writing) have subscribed. Article 11 of the Convention states that "[e]ach Contracting Party shall, as far as possible and appropriate, adopt economically sound measures that act as incentives for the conservation and sustainable use of biological diversity."

Summary

What can we conclude about biodiversity's economic importance and the prospects for generating biodiversity-based income? Clearly biodiversity's importance is great, in the sense that it has been and remains a key contributor to human well-being. We understand enough of this contribution for its magnitude to be clear, although there are probably many aspects that are still invisible to us. John Donne, an English metaphysical poet of the seventeenth century, wrote that

> No man is an island, entire of itself; every man is a piece of the continent, a part of the maine; if a clod be washed away by the sea, Europe is the less, as well as if a promontory were, as well as if a manor of thy friends or thine own were; Any man's death diminishes me, because I am involved in mankind; And therefore never send to know for whom the bell tolls: It tolls for thee.[3]

To parallel John Donne's well-known quotation, no species is an island, entire of itself, not even *Homo sapiens*. Any species' extinction may diminish us, because we depend on many species. In the end, the loss of an apparently small and unimportant group of species could well threaten the provision of ecosystem services essential to humanity. The distinguished biologist E. O. Wilson once said of microbes, "We need them but they don't need us." This is why many scientists see a serious risk in the current rate of species extinction: they cannot be precise about the dangers involved but nonetheless believe that the risk of costly consequences is real.

A look at the extinction of the passenger pigeon can give this point some substance. When Europeans first arrived in America, the passenger pigeon was probably the most abundant bird in the country. Its population was estimated in billions. It traveled around in flocks of hundreds of thousands—flocks so big that their passing darkened the sky for many minutes at a time. By 1914 they were extinct, annihilated by a combination of hunting and destruction of

---

3. Quoted in Hemingway's famous novel *For Whom the Bell Tolls.*

their habitat. It seemed unbelievable that an animal so abundant could be reduced to extinction so fast.

A possible connection between this extinction and the emergence of Lyme disease has recently been proposed. A 1998 letter to *Science* made the following suggestion (Blockstein 1998):

> There is another possible twist to the complicated ecological chain of events presented by Clive G. Jones et al. (Reports, 13 Feb., p. 1023) whereby the incidence of Lyme disease might increase following population increases of mice allowed by a big mast year of acorns. A major competitor of deer and mice for these bumper crops has been absent from the eastern deciduous forests for a century. The extinct passenger pigeon (*Ectopistes migratorius*) was a nomadic wanderer that specialized on a diet of the superabundant, but unpredictable, crops of mast. With a population estimated at 2 to 5 billion, concentrated in enormous flocks, passenger pigeons congregated wherever there were huge crops of mast. The birds were so efficient at denuding the woods of nuts that many observers noted that native wildlife and feral hogs could not find sufficient food after a pigeon flock had passed through. Is it possible that, in the presence of passenger pigeons, the population explosions of mice in mast years, reported by Jones et al., would have been less likely? Could the outbreaks of Lyme disease in the late 20th century have been a delayed consequence of the extinction of the passenger pigeon?

The point here is that with the pigeon's demise, acorns and beechnuts, an important part of its diet, became more available to other nut-eating animals, including mice. Abundant acorn crops always lead to increases in the population of mice, which are the main breeding ground and hosts of the parasites that cause Lyme disease. It is reasonable, then, that the population of Lyme disease vectors also increased. The disease vectors transfer from mice to deer, which browse in the same forests and on the same foods. Obviously, they also cross into territory used by humans. So the extinction of passenger pigeons could have been instrumental in causing the spread of Lyme disease to humans.

This illustrates well the extraordinary complexity of the web of life, of the connections between different species, and between species and human welfare. No one could reasonably have anticipated this connection between passenger pigeons and Lyme disease. No analysis of the consequences of the pigeon's loss could have anticipated such an outcome. Indeed, the bird was so abundant that no one would likely have predicted that human activity could drive it to extinction.

An economically critical question that arises from these observations is, Can this importance be reflected in a commensurate income yielded by the conservation and use of biodiversity? In essence much of what biodiversity contributes is, or has traditionally been, a public good. Its contribution to the functioning of natural ecosystems is nonexcludable and nonrival, as is its insurance value. And knowledge is the quintessential public good. In spite of the overwhelming "public-ness" of much that biodiversity offers us, there is some prospect of commercializing a limited part. Some of the services provided by natural ecosystems can be privatized and sold, generating a return to the conservation of the biodiversity that supports them. In the case of knowledge, the prospect of commercialization rests on the ability to establish intellectual property rights that will effectively privatize some of the public-good aspects of its insurance and knowledge functions. Probably the most fundamental of these functions, like basic scientific research and development, will never be privatized and will thrive only with financial support via other mechanisms.

Chapter 7

Valuation

Our societies depend on the services of natural ecosystems for their existence. But does this importance translate into economic value? Are these services valuable in an economic sense?

Intuitively it may seem that the answer must be yes. In fact, the matter is not so simple as our intuition suggests. Economics is more concerned with *prices* than with *values* or *importance;* the distinction is sharp and will be clarified below.

Oscar Wilde once remarked that a cynic is someone who knows the price of everything and the value of nothing. Economics is cynical in this sense, although this is probably all to the good. Prices that arise from market transactions are important and, in some sense, objective information. Many concepts of value, on the other hand, are subjective.[1]

For a start, we need to be clear that the price of a good does not

---

1. Maynard Keynes, one of the most famous and influential economists, commented, "We have to remain poor because it does not 'pay' to be rich. We destroy the beauty of the countryside because the unappropriated splendors of nature have no economic value. We are capable of shutting off the sun and the stars because they have no economic value." Keynes's comment shows that although economics is cynical, this is not true of all economists. Quoted in Skiddelsky 1992.

reflect its importance in any overall social or philosophical sense. Very unimportant goods can be valued more highly by the market than very important goods, in the sense of having higher prices. The classic illustration of this is the diamonds-and-water paradox: water is clearly more important to human society than diamonds are, yet diamonds trade in the market at prices far in excess of those fetched by water. Why?

This question perplexed economists through the eighteenth and nineteenth centuries until its resolution by Alfred Marshall. Marshall's answer was simple and is by now part of common knowledge: price is set by supply as well as demand. The market price is the price at which the amount supplied is also the amount demanded. In the case of water, the supply (at least in Marshall's time) was so large as to exceed the amount that could possibly be demanded at any price. Consequently the price was zero: water was free. Now, of course, the demand for water has increased greatly because of population growth and rising prosperity, while the supply has remained roughly constant, so that water is no longer free. In the case of diamonds, which are naturally scarce, the desire for ownership always exceeded that which could be accommodated naturally. The market price was high as a result of competition for the few diamonds available.

So, in summary, the fact that something is important does not ensure that its price is high. If, like water in nineteenth-century England, something is naturally abundant, then this will keep down its price.

Food in the industrial countries is another good example of this point. Agricultural systems are sufficiently productive that the needs of the populations in industrial countries can easily be met, and consequently food prices are not high. Indeed, the problem with food in the advanced countries has recently been too much rather than too little production, with farmers complaining of low prices. But food is nevertheless essential to life.

For both water and food, it is likely that if the amounts available were to decrease, their prices would rise substantially. If there really were not enough food to go around in the industrial countries, we would all be willing to spend a large fraction of our incomes to try to get enough for our families, in which case there would be a lot of money chasing relatively little food, and prices would be very different. The same is true of water. So the present prices reflect present supply conditions. They tell us nothing about how things would be if a lot less were available. In discussing the returns to land fertility, David Ricardo, a famous nineteenth-century British economist, put it this way (1911):

> The labour of nature is paid, not because she does much, but because she does little. In proportion as she becomes niggardly in her gifts, she exacts a greater price for her work. Where she is munificently beneficent, she always works gratis.

This observation has considerable relevance to the issues we are exploring. For an example, let's consider it in terms of the possibility of obtaining returns from biodiversity via bioprospecting, which we looked at in Chapter 6. In bioprospecting a company is evaluating compounds derived from different organisms (plants, insects, animals) as possible leads in the design of drugs or agriculturally valuable commodities. Some of the discussion of the earnings potential of bioprospecting has focused on the value of conserving one more plant or insect for investigation—in other words, it has asked the following question: What is it worth to conserve one plant that would otherwise go extinct, so that we can test the value of the compounds in it? The answer of some analysts is very little indeed (Simpson, Sedjo, et al. 1996). This conclusion rests on the assumption that, in the absence of information from tests on chemicals extracted from them, most plants are equivalent in value. Effectively they are all seen as substitutes for one another from this viewpoint, as there are millions of plants species, more than can easily be assessed in any reasonable time. This approach suggests that there is really no shortage of plant species for prospecting purposes. If this were indeed the situation, then we would have another situation like the diamond-water paradox: the value of an extra plant to be conserved would be negligible, even though the total value of all plants as a source of information might be very large. Loss of a single species might have a zero economic cost because there are more species than we need, even though the loss of many species would have a great cost.

In fact this analysis depends heavily on the assumption that all plant or animal or insect species are equivalent from the perspective of a bioprospector, so that we have many more of them than we can use. In reality there are plants that are more likely to be productive of pharmacologically active compounds than others, so the social value of conserving them could be great.

The abundance of food in industrial countries and its low price was noted as another illustration of the diamond-water paradox. Of course, in many developing countries, people die from malnutrition and starvation. How is this compatible with low food prices? Because the populations of these countries cannot afford to compete for food on world markets. Markets are institutions where, as a famous economist once put it, you vote with your dollars. The populations of developing countries, having few dollars, are disenfranchised in this vote.

This leads naturally to another important aspect of prices: they reflect the distribution of income, the existing social order. To continue with the same example, if all the people of Asia and Africa were much wealthier, they would compete with you and me for the world's food output, and consequently food prices would probably be higher. Going back to diamonds, in a world without affluent people the prices of luxury goods such as diamonds would be a lot lower. The reason, of course, is that the distribution of income affects the demands for many goods and therefore their prices. In general, an increase in the income level of a group will increase the demand for goods that they want and so increase the prices of those goods.

What, then, does the market price of a good reflect if it does not reflect importance? It reflects what the good is worth to what we call the "marginal buyer." The marginal buyer is the buyer who is on the verge of not buying the good, the buyer who would drop out if the price were to rise only a small amount. There will typically be many people buying a good for whom that good is worth more than they actually pay. The difference between the price that they pay for a unit of a good and the maximum they would be willing to pay is called their *consumer surplus*. The people who are willing to pay more than the market price and who are enjoying consumer surplus do not determine the market price; it is the buyers who may drop out of the market who do this. There is an analogy here with the legendary swing voters who determine an election outcome. The market price of a good does not tell us how important that good is to society, nor how much some of the people buying it may be willing and able to pay rather than go without. It tells us what it is worth to the "swing buyer," or what economists call the "marginal buyer."

In spite of these qualifications, the market price of a good is a very important and informative number. It tells us how much society would gain if a little more of the good were made available. Why? Because a small increase in the supply would not change the price much; the new buyers would be people who valued the good at about the present price. If they valued it at more than the present price, they would already be buyers. If they valued it a lot less, then a small drop in price would not bring them in. In other words, if a bit more of a good were available to society, then in a market economy the extra would sell at the current market price and be consumed by people who value it at that price. Accepting for the moment the premise that the value of the good to society is the value to those of its members benefiting from the good,[2] this sets its social value at the market price.

To return to water and Marshall, if more water had been made available to the United Kingdom in the nineteenth century, there would have been no gain to society. The supply was sufficient, so extra water was of no value. Of course, this does not mean that society could have survived the loss of a large part of its water supply. But if the water supply had been a lot less, then the price would not have been zero and the market would have indicated a positive value for water. In summary,

> The price of a good tells us how much society would gain (or lose) if a little more (or less) of the good were made available. This is the economic meaning of *value*.

A key aspect of this interpretation is that price tells us about the value of having a little more (or less) of a good. It does not tell us anything about the importance of having a lot more or a lot less. So

---

2. This rests on a utilitarian political philosophy. It sees the good of society as the totality of the well-being of its members. Society has no goals or values not reflected in those of its members.

the prices of water and food tell us about the values of having a little more or less of each, but emphatically not about the values of having a lot less.

Why is this issue of marginal changes relevant to us? What is the point of this focus on small changes, on what economists call "marginal changes"? The answer is that these are generally the kinds of changes that are under consideration when individuals or policy makers are making decisions.[3] The farmer's decision to plant particular crops will not have a big effect on the supply of food. His decision is typically about increasing the output of one crop a little by cutting back on another. He is considering trade-offs between different crops and their impact on his earnings. For these decisions, which affect the availability of only a small amount to society, prices convey the right information. They indicate the social values of small changes in the availability of goods. If farmers and firm managers use these as guides in choosing what to produce, then they will be aligning their choices with what is socially desirable.

Now to return to the issue of valuation. If there were market prices for the services provided by natural ecosystems, then these prices would provide an obvious basis for valuing them. Thus we could value the carbon sequestration services of forests or the water purification services of watersheds by setting market prices for them. We could also place some value on their biodiversity-support roles by looking at the market prices of ecotourism and bioprospecting. From these numbers we could try to compute values for the forest as a whole or for the watershed as a whole.

Typically we value an asset at the present discounted value of the services that it will provide in the future. Corporations, for example, are usually valued at the present discounted value of their estimated future earnings for acquisition or investment purposes. The present discounted value of future services is a number computed by adding together the values of all the future services that will ever be provided, after scaling down the values of the future services by numbers called *discount factors*. Discount factors allow for the fact that

---

3. Policy makers sometimes make decisions that have more than a marginal effect on output levels, as, for example, in agricultural policy choices. In such cases prices are not a good guide to the appropriateness of the alternatives.

investments can earn interest. At 5 percent a year, $100 set aside today will be worth $105 a year hence. Consequently, we can say that $105 a year ahead has a present value of $100 and in present-value calculations scale it down by a discount factor of 100/105. (Chapter 9 will look at this practice and its implications in more detail.) So according to this reasoning, we could value a watershed at the present discounted value of the watershed services that it will provide in the future. We could likewise value a forest at the present discounted value of its carbon sequestration and biodiversity-support services and its recreational services.

Note, of course, that such valuations are incomplete. Natural ecosystems usually provide services for which there are no markets and so no market prices. These will therefore be omitted from calculations that are based entirely on market prices. At best, therefore, computations based on market prices will give lower bounds for the values of natural systems. However, as we have seen in some of the examples in earlier chapters, even these lower bounds can be strikingly high, high enough to generate action for conservation. When there are no markets and so no market prices, we have to turn to a range of nonmarket valuation techniques to assess the value to society of somewhat more or less of an environmental service.

Nonmarket Valuation

Economists have developed many techniques for valuing goods and services for which there is no market. In many cases this research has been motivated by the desire to better understand the economic value of the natural environment. However, similar valuation problems arise with the public sector; it is natural, in judging the contribution of state and local governments to our economies, to ask about the values of education, law and order, and public health, all of which are substantially provided by nonmarket mechanisms. There are several very ingenious ways of placing a value on services for which there is no market price, and next we review some of these.

Hedonic Indices

Perhaps the most convincing approach to nonmarket valuation is the use of what economists have called *hedonic price indices*. The name probably merits an explanation. *Hedonic* clearly has the same linguistic root as *hedonism,* which we associate with the pursuit of pleasure. And that is exactly the point: a hedonic index tracks which aspects of a good or service are particularly pleasing to consumers and influence their overall valuation. This is best explained by an example. Suppose we want to value the fertility of soil. Soil fertility is not a good that is bought and sold in a market, so we cannot just look up the price. However, farms are bought and sold, so we could collect data on farm prices, calculate the prices per acre of the farmland, and then also collect data on the quality of the soil on these farms. Next we would correlate the land price per acre with the quality of the soil and with other important attributes of the land to see how much the fertility of the soil adds to the price of the land. So indirectly we have estimated a price for soil fertility. We have found how it and other characteristics of land affect the values users place on land and so how they contribute to the market price of land.

Securities analysts perform the same type of analysis daily when they ask how the volatility of a stock's earnings affects its market price. There is no market for volatility directly, so they look for comparable stocks with different records of earnings volatility and then attribute the difference to the volatility differences. Indirectly they are placing a market value on volatility. The same technique is used to place a value on intangibles such as views. What is the value of a beautiful view? To answer this, find two comparable houses, one with and one without views, and compare their prices. The difference reflects the value of the view in the marketplace. Real estate appraisers are practicing hedonic valuations whenever they appraise a property by assessing how much each of its attributes contributes to its market value.

All these examples are oversimplified to make the point clear. In practice one would rarely find two houses identical except for the view to be valued. In this case we do the same thing but by a more roundabout route. We will relate the prices of many houses to the attributes of those houses, including size, view, quality, neighborhood, and other variables. We will use statistical techniques that will tell us how much of the variation in house prices is due to the variation in each characteristic. From these we will separate out the part of the variation in prices that is due to differences in views. Indirectly, we put a price on the view.

The same holds true for analysis of stock prices and farm prices. There is a general principle at work here. The price of a good reflects the valuations people place on all of its characteristics. In the case of a house these are size, location, quality, views, and many others. An important part of economic and market research is the study of how each of these characteristics contributes to the value that consumers place on the overall package. These techniques sometimes allow us to value properties for which there is no market. However, for this approach to work there has to be a product for which there is a market and in which the characteristic at issue is embedded. So if we want to use this as a way of valuing nonmarketed ecosystem services, then we can apply it only to cases in which they contribute directly to something that is marketed.

Replacement Costs

Another possibility, perhaps less general, is the use of replacement costs as a way of valuing a natural service. This can work even if there is no marketed service to which the natural service contributes. Again, the best way to start is with an example. In Chapter 3 we looked at the case of New York's decision to preserve the Catskill watershed. In that case the city had an alternative to restoring the watershed: replacing it with a filtration plant. This would have cost about $6–8 billion plus operating costs and eventually replacement costs. Call the total $9 billion for simplicity. Can we say that because the cost of replacing the watershed would have been $9 billion, that is its value? Certainly this is a tempting strategy.

There are pros and cons to this approach to valuation. As in the cases in which there are markets for some of the services of an ecosystem, we can reach at best a partial valuation of the watershed via this route: a filtration plant replaces only a small part of what a watershed does. A filtration plant does not sequester carbon or support biodiversity or provide recreational opportunities. It does not even purify water as well as a natural watershed. So at best we can reach a partial, lower-bound estimate of the cost of replacing the ecosystem's services.

Another argument goes in the opposite direction: We will not always choose to replace something that is defective—the cost of replacement could be too high. In the New York watershed case, nonreplacement was not an option: the city needs drinking water. Suppose instead that the Catskills had just been providing recreational services to the city, and that the replacement of those services was at issue. And suppose that the cost of replacing them with equivalent services and facilities was billions of dollars. In all probability the city would have decided not to replace the recreational services of the Catskills. It would have decided that at the cost of several billions, recreation was a luxury that people could do without. In this case the replacement cost would not be a proper indicator of the value of the service. Replacement cost can be a good indicator only if it is a cost that will be incurred if a replacement is needed.

The same principle operates in many other contexts. We often decide not to replace something that is lost or broken because it is not worth the cost. But as noted earlier, in the case of a watershed supplying a critical life-support service, nonreplacement is not a possibility. However, even in the New York case we cannot legitimately say that the value of the watershed is $9 billion, as in fact the city never chose to pay that amount: it restored the watershed at a much lower cost of $1–2 billion. We can say that the city saved $9 billion through environmental conservation—it allowed the city to attain its goal of potable water without spending $9 billion on a filtration plant. Perhaps we can even say that environmental conservation enriched the city by $9 billion minus $1.5 billion, the cost of watershed restoration. This is a net enrichment of $7.5 billion. But this is not the same as placing a value on the watershed: it is valuing the consequences of a conservation policy.

In summary, assessing replacement cost is not a convincing way of valuing natural ecosystems and the services they provide. Replacements rarely replace all the services coming from the original system, so that they can capture only a part of the value. But more fundamentally, replacement cost is not a proper estimate of the value unless the cost is incurred. There will be cases in which this does not happen; these are cases in which replacement will be too expensive to make sense.

Replacement costs are certainly interesting, indeed essential, information in the context of evaluating conservation policies, particularly for essential services for which a replacement would surely be needed were the original system to fail. The replacement cost is a benchmark that decision makers need to have in mind as they evaluate conservation and restoration options. But, again, this does not make it a good estimate of the economic value of a system or service.

To underscore this point, let's look at one more example: oil. Oil is close to essential to industrial economies. If all oil were to vanish tomorrow, it could (with difficulty) be replaced. We could, for example, extract oil from coal through complex industrial processes at a cost of about $40 to $50 per barrel.[4] Or we could extract it from shale or from tar sands, at similar prices. When I began writing this book in late 1998, the price of oil was $18 per barrel, although in early 2000 it had reached about $30 per barrel and in spring it had dipped to about $24. As its replacement cost is at least $40 per barrel, does this mean that its value is $40 per barrel? Clearly not: its value is its market price. Currently the supply is sufficiently abundant that there is no prospect of having to pay the replacement cost. However, if the supply were to start running out, then the market price would rise toward the replacement cost, which would become more relevant as an indicator of value.

Travel Costs

Let's briefly look at another approach to valuing environmental services that are not marketed. This is the travel-cost method. The idea is to estimate how much people value an environmental asset by seeing what costs they will incur to visit it. The travel-cost method has typically been applied in the cases of national parks and ecotourism facilities. The basic idea is simple: if I am willing to incur costs of, say, $500 to visit a park and spend time there, then being there must provide me with benefits that I value at least that much. It must be worth at least $500 to me. We can think of the access costs as a price that people pay to get to the park.

Across all visitors there will be many different access costs, so that

---

4. A barrel is 42 U.S. gallons.

different people are in effect paying different prices for access to the park. Some may live locally and incur costs of only a few dollars; others may live far away and have to travel for hours at great expense to get there. If there are many different implied prices, then which do we use to value the facility? Which can act like a market price?

Recall that market price tells us the value of having a little more or less of a good. In fact, there is no exact equivalent of this for a park: a park is a public good, and for the reasons indicated in Chapter 2, there will generally not be a single price that represents its social value. In such cases we have to add up the values attributed to it by all of its users and take this sum as the valuation of the services it provides. So the sum of the travel costs incurred to visit the park would be the natural indicator of the value of providing slightly more of the park's services.

Contingent Valuation

Market prices, hedonic prices, travel costs, and replacement costs as methods of valuing the services of natural systems have an important feature in common: they are based on actual transactions. Hedonic prices are derived from market prices. Travel costs reflect real transactions. And replacement costs, used properly, reflect a cost that will be incurred if replacement is needed.

The remaining method of valuation, used when none of the others is possible, is called *contingent valuation*. In essence it involves asking a carefully structured sample of people what value they place on a natural asset and then using those data to extrapolate to the population as a whole. The questions posed have to be carefully designed for the answers to have any validity. With this caveat, such methods have been widely used for estimating the value of lost natural amenities, particularly in high-profile lawsuits such as the *Exxon Valdez* case.

It is fair to say that most economists feel more comfortable with valuations based on actual transactions rather than those given in response to hypothetical questions, however carefully constructed. Intuitively there seems to be a big difference between answering a survey question asking what you would be willing to pay for something, and actually paying for it. In spite of such reservations, this approach has given quite good predictions of what people might pay in situations when it has been possible to compare contingent valuation estimates of what people might pay with what they have subsequently paid.

In summary, economists would ideally like to value ecosystem services by attaching market prices to them or by deriving prices for them from market transactions. This cannot always be done. But even when it is possible, the resulting market-based valuations need not reflect the social importance of the services or the extent of the losses that we would suffer if these services were removed. Market-based prices tell us the value of a small amount (more or less) of a service to society and do not indicate the overall contribution of the service. Operationally, this is usually fine as small changes in availability are generally at issue. To summarize again,

---

Economists would ideally like to value ecosystem services by attaching market prices to them or by deriving prices for them from market transactions. Market-based prices tell us the value of a small amount (more or less) of a service to society and do not indicate the overall contribution of the service.

Unfortunately, some of the human impacts on important ecosystems are far from small. Overfishing is radically changing marine food chains. Nitrogen fertilizers have already more than doubled natural nitrogen concentrations. We have significantly increased atmospheric concentrations of carbon dioxide and other greenhouse gases. We are driving species extinct at perhaps one thousand times the natural rate. In such cases market prices, even if they exist, will seriously underestimate the economic value lost by this destruction.

Why will market prices give an underestimate? Because typically the price of a good or service rises as it becomes scarcer. This is particularly true of goods and services that are essential to human welfare, such as food, water, and clean air. As noted above, if food or water were scarce in affluent countries, then most of us would spend a significant proportion of our incomes ensuring adequate supplies for our families. In such a world, prices of food, water, and access to clean air would rise dramatically, and the prices of other goods would fall as there was less left to spend on them.

Are there any economic measures that would more effectively capture the impact of a significant loss of a natural life-support system? For example, can we talk sensibly of the value of preserving the climate system intact or of the value of preserving biodiversity? In principle there are ways of doing this. However, it will never make sense to ask about the value that we would lose if an entire and irreplaceable life-support system were irrevocably damaged. If it is indeed a life-support system, then its loss would lead to the end of life, and to put an economic value on that would seem foolish and inappropriate.

Recently there have been attempts to apply nonmarket and nonmarginal valuation methods to assess the economic value of the biosphere in a comprehensive way. Perhaps the most famous or notorious of these is that of Costanza, d'Arge, et al. (1997), who reported an estimate of about $30 trillion for the total value of the Earth's ecosystem services, a number in excess of the planetary national income. Unfortunately this study was flawed, so seriously as to be of no use, precisely because its authors were not sensitive to the point just made: it does not make sense to ask about the value of replacing a life-support system. One economist described the numbers resulting from this study as "a serious underestimate of infinity" (Toman 1998).

Nonmarginal Values

Could we assess a value on the loss of a significant part, but not all, of a life-support system? Theoretically we might be able to do this, but it is difficult. Take a concrete case, water. Suppose we want to value the consequences of a change in the hydrological cycle resulting from a change in the climate system, and that this hydrological change would substantially reduce, but not eliminate, water supplies to large regions of the Earth. Could we evaluate the consequences of this hydrological change by means of economic techniques? To do so we would have to know how much the price of water would rise as its supply falls—in economic terms, we would have to know the demand curve for water. This is not easy. As the water price rises because of scarcity, production, food prices, income levels, and many other economic variables would change. All these as well as other variables would affect the demand for water, so that estimating how its price would move along a trajectory of declining supply would be immensely difficult. To date, there have been no convincing studies assessing the economic value of preventing significant losses in global life-support systems, although in principle we do know how to carry out such a valuation.

The conclusion that emerges from this analysis is that economics probably cannot really value the services of the Earth's life-support systems in any way other than by means of market prices, which only indicate the value of a small change in their availability.

Some people might find this disappointing. But in fact we should not be disappointed with this limited ability to value ecosystem services. This disappointment typically comes from a feeling that conservation of natural ecosystems matters, and that the prospects for conservation can be improved by attaching impressive values to the systems to be conserved. There may be some truth in this, but, in reality,

> Valuation is neither necessary nor sufficient for conservation. We conserve much on which we do not place economic value, and we do not conserve much that we value economically.

What, then, is the economic prerequisite for conservation? It lies in incentives—to conserve systems, we must give their owners incentives to conserve them. We must make conservation more attractive than any other use. Conserving forests must be more attractive than clearing them to plant coffee or bananas or cocoa beans. To achieve this, we have to translate some of the social importance of ecosystem services into income and ensure that this income accrues to the owners of the ecosystems as a reward for their conservation. This is a theme that has recurred many times in previous chapters. It is the key theme, the single most important theme, in the conservation of the ecosystems that support human societies. Providing the right incentives is not the same as valuing the services: we can provide incentives without valuing the services, and we can value the services without providing incentives for conserving them. In fact, valuation may sometimes be a by-product of providing the incentives. If we manage to establish a market in an ecosystem service, as discussed in Chapters 3 through 6, then we have a price for it and thus a basis for valuing it. And markets are probably the best ways of providing conservation incentives. So, logically, incentives come before valuation. In summary:

> Incentives are critical for conservation. Valuation is not necessary for establishing the correct incentives, although correct incentives may provide a mechanism for valuation.

There is an exception to the general statement that valuation is neither necessary nor sufficient for conservation. This statement is true insofar as conservation decisions are guided by market forces. But some such decisions are a part of the political process. The recent decision to attempt to restore much of the Florida Everglades ecosystem to its original state is an example of a high-profile political conservation decision. Ratification of the Kyoto Protocol—which, as we have seen, would be a key step forward in many areas—has to be carried out at the political level. In political decisions, cost-benefit analysis can be influential. A cost-benefit analysis requires the enumeration and evaluation of the benefits from conserving a natural ecosystem. In this process, placing values on the services provided by the system is a necessary step.

When noneconomists talk of the value of nature and of nature's services, they often mean something quite different from the market prices of these services or from the social gains of having a small amount more or less. This was presumably the point of the remark by Oscar Wilde quoted at the start of this chapter. Here, value is clearly meant to be morally superior to price. What, exactly, is this alternative sense of value? The *Oxford English Dictionary* gives several senses of the word *value:* "1 worth, desirability or utility. 2 amount of money or goods for which a thing can be exchanged in the open market. 3 one's principles or standards: one's judgment of what is valuable or important in life." Clearly the economic definition corresponds to the second of these meanings. Oscar Wilde probably had in mind the third—one's principles or standards. All of these meanings have relevance to natural systems. Natural systems can be desirable for reasons other than their economic contributions, and indeed this may be related to the basic moral principles through which we choose to relate to the natural environment.

For example, some people believe that natural systems, and animals in particular, have a right to exist quite independently of their contributions to human societies. One may take the view that tigers have the right to exist even if they contribute nothing directly to human welfare or indeed even if they inflict damage on human societies. The same argument can be made for less charismatic organisms such as insects and fish, though in these cases the argument typically gets less attention. Part of what is at issue here is what economists have called *existence value:* people attribute value to the fact that something exists, even if they do not expect to see it or use it. And in general we are more likely to attribute existence value to species that are clearly appealing or magnificent or impressive since they are more likely to elicit our sympathy. To some degree such values can be captured by the contingent valuation method mentioned earlier: by the careful use of structured questionnaires designed to elicit what the respondents are willing to pay for the preservation of a species.

Another view is that as a matter of principle we have a responsibility to pass on the Earth to the next generation in as good a state as that in which we received it from our predecessors. From this perspective the Earth is not ours to do with as we wish: we hold it in trust for our successors, just as our predecessors held it in trust for us. We are the stewards and not the owners of nature's beneficence. It is not ours to dispose of, but ours to conserve and pass on.

Perhaps some of the most important contributions of nature to human welfare relate to its impact on the human psyche. History provides many examples attesting to this role of nature. Painting, poetry, and literature draw on the beauty of nature, and the same attributes of the natural world that inspire the arts daily renew the humanity of millions of our fellow citizens and provide them with inspiration. E. O. Wilson has argued (1998) that we have an innate and inherited affection for the natural world because it is the context in which we evolved and in which our capabilities and instincts were tested and sharpened. We are made for it and it is made for us in the sense that it is where we come from and the milieu in which we have evolved over millions of years. Our genetic makeup changes slowly, and we are still adapted to the world in which our hunter-gatherer ancestors lived and died. Wilson terms this *biophilia:* an innate and inherited love of and dependence on the natural world.

Some of this value can be reflected in economic valuation. The satisfaction we get from nature-based recreation is in part a reflection of Wilson's concept of biophilia. Consequently the amounts we spend on such recreation and on ecotourism are at least a partial reflection of this value.

None of the noneconomic aspects of natural systems' value in any way contradict the economic aspects of value. Value is an inherently multidimensional property. A system or species may have little measurable economic value yet have immense value as a source of aesthetic uplift. Alternatively, as in the case of tigers or whales, we may feel a profound and compelling desire to protect them without any clear economic justification. There is no problem with this. In making decisions society has to take into account all aspects of its interactions with the natural world. Economists do not claim that economic aspects are unique or even primary.

Economic aspects are, however, probably easier to communicate and agree on than the other aspects of value. Many people feel that the extinction of any animal species is a grave loss, whatever its economic utility: species have evolved as part of the natural world of which we are all a part and have a right to a continued existence in that world. To these people this is a moral imperative. But many other people disagree, and convincing them otherwise would be exceedingly difficult. The issue turns on matters of personal values, one's judgment of what is important or valuable in life (to quote the dictionary definition of *value* given above). It is notoriously difficult to reconcile differences in this sphere.

In contrast, there is a good chance of reaching agreement on matters of economic importance or value. If I claim that it is economically important to preserve certain systems and you disagree, then we should be able to resolve our differences. We are disagreeing over numbers and not over principles of morality. Such disagreements rarely go to the heart of someone's being and touch deep chords. It should be possible for us to sit down and review the numbers in a

noncontentious manner and at the very least delimit the range of disagreements to particular numbers and the way they have been com-
piled. So there is, in general, more prospect of agreement on the economic dimensions of value than on the noneconomic dimensions, at
least in societies with a wide range of personal ethical value systems
and attitudes toward the natural world. In this context it may make
sense to focus on the economic aspect first, in the hope that sufficient
agreement can be reached there to reach an agreement on the merits
of conservation. If we can agree to conserve something for economic
reasons, then we need not touch on the fact that I think that it should
be conserved anyway and you do not.

A final point about economic incentives relative to other ways of
bringing about environmental conservation: loosely speaking, we
can classify the ways of persuading people to conserve the natural
environment in three categories. One, people may make choices that
conserve the environment because society instructs them to do so and
will penalize them if they disobey. This is the essence of the regulatory approach, the one most widely used to date. Two, people may
make choices that conserve the environment because they believe as
a matter of principle that this is how they should act; it is consistent
with their views on what matters in life and how one should run
one's life. Environmental activists are usually in this category. Three,
people may choose environmentally conservative strategies because
these options are in their economic self-interest. The prices they face
fully reflect the social costs of their actions, and they are naturally led
by the invisible hand to make conservative choices.

Which of these is most appealing? Which is most likely to be successful when applied on a large scale? This second question is critical. As noted in the first chapter, scientists argue that we can maintain the integrity of essential planetary systems only through large
changes in our impacts on them, and in the ways in which we interact with them (Vitousek, Mooney, et al. 1997; Lubchenco 1998).
Whatever method we choose for changing our interactions with
them must, therefore, be applied on a large scale to many aspects of
our activity.

In this context, the use of economic incentives stands out. Most
of us would not be comfortable with a massive expansion of the reg-

ulatory approach, with its complement of *thou shalt not*s, fines, inspections, and other mechanisms of enforcement. Such an approach would almost certainly generate a strong political backlash. Ideally we would rely on people doing the right thing for the sake of doing the right thing, the approach of the committed environmentalist. But historically this has not worked, and there are no reasons to expect a change in the near future. More public education on the main issues will certainly help but is most unlikely to solve the problem. Appeals to the best in human nature have rarely, if ever, transformed a society. In contrast, economic incentives have worked in the great majority of the areas where they have been applied. They lack the discordant political overtones of regulation and are effective. They tie together doing good and doing well. They replace the stick with the carrot. They will have to be the main mechanism for preserving planetary systems, but we need to orient them more in this direction. We need, in the words of E. O. Wilson (1993), "to give the invisible hand of market economics a green thumb." There will certainly be cases in which incentives fail and regulations are needed (more on this in the next chapter), but they nevertheless must be our first line of defense.

Summary

This chapter has covered a wide range of concepts, so to summarize:

- The natural economic sense of value is the market price of a good, or the price derived from a market price.
- This price does not make any statement about the overall importance of a good and, in particular, does not tell us anything about how much would be lost if much of the good were unavailable.
- Market price tells us the value of a little more or less of a good or service to society.
- Valuation is not necessary for conservation; conservation depends on incentives. Markets can provide incentives and also a value. The value in this case is a by-product of what really matters: the incentives. One exception to this is in the case of a cost-benefit analysis of a conservation project as a part of a political decision-making process.

- There are other senses of value that need not be correlated with economic value, as defined in the first item above. It may be that the economic value of an ecosystem is easier to agree on than the other values. It may therefore make sense, in terms of minimizing discord, to focus first on economic values.
- Providing the appropriate economic incentives has to be our principal tool in seeking to conserve what is important in the natural environment.

Chapter 8

Policies and Institutions

We can reasonably hope to create markets in the services of important ecosystems in several cases. Earlier chapters have discussed potential markets for water purification services, carbon sequestration services, the aspects of biodiversity that generate a demand for ecotourism, and possibly some other aspects of biodiversity, including those that generate leads for new pharmaceutical products. This is a good beginning. If we were to follow up on each of these possibilities, we would go a long way toward transforming human interactions with the biosphere in a constructive direction.

But it would still leave many ecosystem services uncovered. One difficulty in creating such markets is the public-good nature of many key services, a problem in creating the incentives needed for their conservation. If we cannot "privatize" nature's services through the marketplace, what other options do we have? What else in the economists' policy toolkit can we use?

Several different approaches are possible. Some operate at the level of national or international policy; others operate through changes in institutions at a smaller scale. The latter are probably easier to implement because they have a lower political profile and are less likely to cause controversy. Of course, because they operate on a smaller scale, they are also able to achieve less. Some are simple in principle and are perhaps not what we traditionally think of as economic policies. They involve changes in organization or in administrative structure. Others involve legal changes, changes in property rights. Still others, such as taxes, subsidies, and tradable permits, are more clearly economic. Let's look at some of these measures.

Organization

One of the simplest approaches, at least conceptually, is to rearrange organizational boundaries. The point underlying this approach is that many of the economic difficulties we face arise from differences between private and social costs and benefits. These mean that the consequences of an action for the broader community are different from those for carrying it out. In some cases we can correct this by redrawing boundaries so as to redefine the groups and communities at issue. Simple agricultural examples provide a good starting point.

Two important services provided to agriculture by natural ecosystems are pollination and pest control (Nabhan and Buchmann 1997; Naylor and Ehrlich 1997). Pollination may occur in many different ways: by bees seeking food from flowers, by the activities of other insects, by windborne exchanges of pollen between plants, and by the actions of birds, bats, and other animals. Many commercially important crops require insect pollination (Daily and Dasgupta 2000).

The problem is, the practices that are intended to control pests tend to destroy both pests and pollinators. The chemical pesticides used to control insect pests in most intensive agricultural systems generally do not discriminate between agriculturally beneficial and harmful insects. One consequence of pesticide use has been a sharp drop in the population of native honeybees and other pollinators in the United States, although other factors have also contributed, in particular development of former wildlands and consequent destruction of habitats and, in the case of bees, infection by parasites. Natural insect pollination is now almost unknown in many areas. In such regions farmers rent bees from beekeepers in other parts of the United States to pollinate their crops.

Ironically, we find the equivalent of an arms race between the pests and the pesticide designers. In many cases, insect pests develop resistance to insecticides, so that their effectiveness drops off sharply after some years of use. Pesticide manufacturers create new products, subsequent generations of pests again become resistant, and the cycle repeats.

An alternative to chemical pesticides is the use of natural predators, which can be a less expensive and, in the long run, more reliable pest-control method. All insects have natural predators, including spiders, other insects, such as ladybugs (which eat aphids), insect-eating birds, bats, and fishes. As in the case of pollinators, many natural predators have been driven out of areas by pesticide usage and habitat loss.

Another reason for the decline in pollinators and in the predators of agricultural pests is the sheer size of fields, which have grown to accommodate equipment and meet the needs of large-scale production. Birds generally do not fly across wide expanses, preferring to move from greenway to greenway. And indeed, the traditional farm was edged by woods and broken up with hedgerows. There is clear evidence that such a structure gives greatly improved natural protection against pests (Thies and Tscharntke 1999). Even in the case of large farming operations, preserving small amounts of natural habitat in the form of woods and copses and providing hedgerows can lead to thriving populations of wildlife. Because they act both as pollinators and as predators of many common pests, this can be a cost-effective approach to pest control and pollination. It may also lead to crops with higher market value, as consumers are often willing to pay more for food grown without pesticides. In the United Kingdom, organic crops now sell for up to three times the price of similar nonorganic crops (*Financial Times* 2000), and one in three of all consumers eat some organic food (*The Independent* 2000). On this point, *The Economist* (2000) reports that "[f]or the past two years, the Anglo-Dutch giant [Unilever] has been running pilot programs with growers to spread expertise [about natural pest management and related issues] around the world. It has found, for example, that natural forest left among its Kenya tea plantations harbours insects that keep nasty bugs in check and act as a windbreak, as well as providing fuel for locals. This technique is now being passed on to the firm's plantations in India."

In some cases business is beginning to see the benefits of such approaches. For example, Sainsburys, one of the largest food retailers in the United Kingdom, now requires its produce growers to use natural pest controls and encourages suppliers to practice integrated pest management (IPM). IPM involves a combination of natural pest controls, annual rotation of crops to minimize the carryover of plant-specific pests from year to year, the mixture of several different crops on adjacent fields to minimize transfer of pests across fields, and the use of pesticides when needed. However, there are obstacles to wider use of these practices. To be effective, natural methods need to be applied throughout a region, not just on isolated farms. Chemical pesticides, either airborne or as runoff, drift across boundaries, harming wildlife in neighboring areas. The farm relying on natural controls will be without either pesticide or pest predators, vulnerable to attack if neighbors use pesticides.

So these policies need to be coordinated on a regional basis. There is a case for districts within which everyone takes the same approach to pest control, because without this coordination all will be forced to resort to the use of pesticides, even if that is not their first choice. Such management regimes can arise naturally, from cooperation between all those involved, or they can be established as part of a policy to minimize pollution from pesticide use.

Another simple example of a need for coordination is also a traditional economic example: beekeepers and apple farmers who are located near each other. Each producer is providing ecosystem services to the other: bees pollinate apple blossoms and apple flowers provide food for bees and assist in honey production. The concept of external effects described in Chapter 2 applies here, even to the extent that each type of farmer will tend to underprovide his output because a part of it is something for which he is not rewarded. The incentives to the beekeeper come only from the sale of honey and those to the apple grower only from the sale of apples. But in fact, each is contributing to the production of the other good.

Suppose now that the two operations were to merge and become one farm, making money from both honey and apples. In this case the incentives would be correct: the manager of the farm would see his profits from apples increase with the scale of beekeeping and vice versa. There would no longer be external effects: they would have been internalized, in economic jargon, by the merger.

This example reflects an important point. There is a general tendency for an organization to expand so as to bring inside the firm all the main external effects that it generates. In New York State, where apple growing is a major agricultural activity, farmers now regularly rent bees from Texan beekeepers to pollinate their trees. A large farmer may pay tens of thousands of dollars for this service, indicating clearly its economic value to him.

Microsoft is a classic example of this phenomenon in a totally different context. Changes in the operating system of personal computers have consequences for those who produce software for Windows-based computers. So Microsoft can generate positive external effects for the producers of Windows-based software through a more robust and powerful operating system with enhanced capabilities, and there is a natural tendency for it to expand and incorporate these producers. But this may ultimately lead to an antitrust problem.

In fact we saw some of this tendency to expand the boundaries of an organization to include closely related entities at work in our discussion of watersheds. The commercial provision of water is producing incentives for the water companies to control their watersheds. There are the same analytical issues underlying these incentives: the watershed produces important externalities for the water company, in that it affects the quality and quantity of water moving downstream, and thus the costs of the water company. So there is a clear case for the water company to control it.

Suppose, for example, that the watershed were forested and controlled by a timber company, and that this company also provided water to a downstream city water company. By policies such as clear-cutting, which lead to soil loss and degradation of the watershed, the timber company will impose costs on the water company; as long as the timber and water companies are separate entities, the timber company will make the wrong decisions with respect to choices affecting water quality. These costs are not reflected in the timber company's own books and thus will not affect its policy. Hence it has an overly strong incentive to clear-cut and no incentive to care for water quality. If the management of the watershed and the provision of water to the city were integrated into one company, the problem would be solved. The integrated company would earn profits from both timber production and the provision of water of drinkable quality, and so would have to balance the gains from extra timber production by clear-cutting against the losses from reduced water quality and increased water-treatment costs. Once again, integration or merger can lead to better coordination. In this case, it replaces a market for water in which the timber company, as manager of the watershed, would be a seller and the water company a buyer. This market is replaced by an internal transaction between two different parts of a single enterprise.

In the orchard-bees example there is something similar: a strictly market-oriented solution would have the beekeeper paying the apple grower for the food his bees derive from the orchard and the apple grower paying for the pollination services of the bees. Merging the two operations means that there is no longer a need for these markets. A new organizational structure has replaced them.

Something very much like this happens with district heating systems, increasingly being used in Scandinavia. Electric power plants heat water and use the steam to drive a turbine and generate electricity. In most power stations the steam emerging from the turbine is still hot and so carries heat energy, yet is vented through a cooling tower. In integrated district heating systems the steam emerging from the turbines of a power plant is used to provide domestic heating and hot water to residences in the neighboring vicinity. The plant not only generates and sells electricity but also manages the domestic heat needs of a district of which it is a part. This leads to far more efficient use of energy because the hot steam that is normally wasted is used to meet domestic demands at no additional energy cost. Again, the key is to integrate power generation and district heating, and so develop a framework for making use of a valuable by-product of one industry in another sector.

Traditionally farmers in Europe countered the loss of soil fertility caused by continued agricultural use through a number of measures. These include manuring fields, alternating crops that increase soil fertility (such as legumes, which "fix" atmospheric nitrogen into organic compounds and so add nitrogen-containing compounds to the soil, with other crops, and allowing fields to go fallow. Since the green revolution, most of these practices have been abandoned. In many cases they were abandoned long before (Tilman 1998). Under high-intensity agriculture, farms specialize in particular crops, planting only wheat or corn or similar crops year after year. The degradation of the soil that naturally results has been countered by the application of fertilizers; in fact, fertilizer use has increased seven times since 1960 and exceeds 7×10^7 tons annually, an amount equal to the total natural production of all nitrogen-containing compounds (Tilman 1998). This intensive use of nitrogen, as noted in Chapter 1, is changing the planetary nitrogen cycle quite fundamentally, and in ways that are causing concern among scientists (Vitousek, Mooney, et al. 1997; Tilman 1998; Matson, Parton, et al. 1997). Livestock farming, once practiced alongside cropping and providing a local source of manure as fertilizer, has broken away and become a separate large-scale business, producing manure on a massive scale and leading to serious disposal problems, with some waste running off into rivers and waterways. Much of this animal waste could be used to restore soil fertility.

Recent reviews in *Nature* (Tilman 1998; Drinkwater, Wagoner, et al. 1998) noted that this specialization and intensification of agriculture has broken what was once the tight, local recycling of nutrients on individual farms. The U.S. Environmental Protection Agency estimates that, in the United States alone, livestock operations generate about 10^3 tons of manure per year, much of it in large-scale operations in which up to a quarter of a million animals are housed in close quarters. They are already causing serious deterioration of water quality in many waterways and estuaries. These concentrated sources of manure are often too far from farms to be economically transported to them, are applied at inappropriately high rates or at the incorrect times if used as manure, or are released into waterways without removing the nitrogen and phosphorus they contain. These nutrients in waste lead to eutrofication of waterways, creating an open nitrogen cycle that is rapidly degrading many other ecosystems.

Of course, there are reasons that farmers and ranchers choose such approaches: highly intensive agriculture earns a higher return than more sustainable and less polluting approaches. And it gives rise to social costs that are not reflected in private costs to farmers: it leads to a use of certain techniques that are excessive from the perspective of society as a whole, nitrogen fertilization being a prime example. One solution, as suggested in Chapter 2, is to tax polluting output or introduce tradable pollution permits to bring the social and private costs of agricultural activity into line. Another is to integrate the different types of agricultural activity so that wastes from animal farming are used by crop growers, simultaneously cutting back both on nitrogen use and on the release of animal wastes.

All these examples illustrate the same point: organizational integration can be crucial in ensuring that all the consequences of actions are carefully considered. Farms that practiced both cropping and animal husbandry had a use for the by-products of animal farming and had natural ways of restoring soil fertility that did not lead to massive losses of nitrogen and other nutrients into the general environment.

With the present organization of agriculture we will have to develop other ways of limiting the release of nitrogen fertilizers into the environment and other ways of managing the massive manure outputs of factory farms. In economic terms, in much the same way as in the earlier example of timber and water companies, integrated farms internalize many of the external effects associated with agriculture. They can use the wastes from animal farming as inputs to crop production rather than disposing of them into the environment.

An interesting and rather different illustration of the practical power of these ideas about organization and integration comes from a story reported in *The Economist*. It concerns a group of hunters who were concerned that the land on which they had traditionally hunted would be used for residential development. To ensure the continuation of their hunting rights, they obtained financing to purchase the land and subdivided it into two sections. On one they built a small number of luxury homes, and on the other they imposed conservation easements guaranteeing that the land would never be developed and would remain forever in its natural state. The easements greatly enhanced the value of the homes, and the hunters were able to sell them for more than the costs of buying the land and construction.

This example again illustrates the internalization of externalities through careful organization. The point is that by imposing conservation easements on the land not developed in order to assure their ability to hunt in perpetuity, the hunters greatly increased the value of the adjacent developed land. They were able to capture this enhanced value for themselves through the construction and sale of houses on the land. Their conservation easements created value for adjacent landowners via social benefits in excess of the private benefits: the private benefit was the continued ability to hunt, and the social benefits included the ability to live next to land that would remain pristine. They were able to capture some of this difference.

The present and earlier examples illustrate the same point: that changes in organizational structure can have a powerful and beneficial impact on incentives. They can align the financial incentives associated with operating businesses and farms with social benefits—in other words, they can allow business to employ the invisible hand, to do well financially by doing good.

This observation connects with a point made in the last chapter: incentives are more important to conservation than valuation. The mergers described in the examples above improve incentives for conservation of ecosystem services without in any way placing explicit values on them. Society can bring about the right decisions from a conservation perspective without ever having to value the services being conserved, by just putting them under the control of the right organizations. Of course, the merged units—the water-cum-timber company, for example—will have to value the ecosystem services for their own decision-making purposes. The company would have to decide how much the integrity of the forest affects the quality of water and then see how this affects its profits, which involves placing a value on the integrity of the forest.

Property Rights

Closely related to the issue of organization is that of property rights. Chapter 2's discussion of external effects touched on this subject, noting that external effects arise from the lack of well-defined property rights in certain environmental assets. This naturally brings up the issue of what are called *common-pool resources*. Many environmental assets and important ecosystems are in this category. Common-pool resources are resources that are, literally, common property, and that consequently are owned by no one. When no one is excluded from using them—that is, they can be used by all without limitation—they are often also called *open-access resources.*

To repeat and indeed emphasize, there are no institutions governing the use of open-access, common-pool resources. Examples are fisheries on the high seas outside of the economic zones of coastal nations, the atmosphere, large inland lakes not owned or regulated by any agency, and grazing lands to which access is open to all livestock owners. In all these cases many users compete for the services of the resource; if this is an ecosystem, then they can compete for the ecosystem goods or services that it provides and may in the process degrade it irreversibly. Commercial fishing is a good and regrettably topical example: fishing fleets from many nations compete for the products of marine ecosystems and in the process have seriously damaged many of them, driving important species close to extinction and damaging, perhaps irreparably, the habitats of bottom-dwelling species through destructive trawling operations.

The economic issues here were discussed briefly in Chapter 2. The point is that in fisheries there is a difference between private and social returns. There is a fixed stock of fish in a fishery at any point of time, so the more of them caught by one boat, the fewer there will be left for others. If I catch more, you will probably catch less. So the social costs of my activities include the cost of others' catching less. This is not a private cost to me; it is, however, a cost to everyone else. The extreme case would occur if I got to the fishing ground first and caught all the available fish. Obviously my success would be at your expense. So again there is a difference between private and social costs.

The same is true of all common-pool resources. In the case of grazing land, grass eaten by my cattle cannot be eaten by yours, so my consumption of the services of this ecosystem is at your expense. There is again a negative external effect from one user to all others.

How should we manage common-pool resources? A part of the answer should be familiar by now: we need to correct the difference between private and social costs. We can do this by taxing the use of the resource. This need not be a tax on the use directly but could be a tax on the inputs that have to be bought to use the common-pool resource—for example, rather than taxing fishing we could tax the sale of fishing boats or nets. Alternatively we could require users of the resource to purchase permits before they have the right to use the common-pool resource, permits that could be traded between different users. Either of these devices would increase the private costs of using the common resource and would therefore bring the private costs into line with the social costs.

Most economists prefer systems in which individuals or businesses own tradable permits, like the one proposed for controlling greenhouse gases under the Kyoto Protocol. With a permit regime there has to be a decision on the acceptable level of use of the common resource, as this determines the number of permits to be sold. In the case of a resource such as a fishery, this decision should be made by a body that can assess the population dynamics of the fish species and the levels of catch that are consistent with their survival. The use of tradable permits goes directly to the heart of the common-pool problem in that it transforms the resource from one to which the entire population has access to one to which only a well-defined group has access. In addition, it ensures that this group can only make limited use of the resource. And, of course, the cost of buying a permit raises the private cost of using the resource to the social level.

Note in passing, and as a connection with the earlier discussion of organizational structures, that if a common-pool resource is used by a monopolist, a single user, then there is no problem of overexploitation or of differences between private and social costs. The reason is simple: the external effects that occur with common-pool resources are between different users; with a single user there can be no such effects. They are internalized, just as in the case of the integration of timber management and water provision in a watershed or integration of apple growing and beekeeping. This illustrates the saying "The monopolist is the conservationist's best friend." The essential point here is that a common-pool resource whose use is monopolized is really no longer a common-pool resource. It is the private property of the monopolist.

Many societies have developed noneconomic mechanisms for regulating the use of common-pool resources. These have ranged from social conventions about what is an appropriate level of use of a common grazing land or stream to complex legal sanctions designed to enforce operation of the resource as if by a single owner. In small, stable medieval societies, for instance, access to grazing lands was open but monitored, with clear norms about what constituted reasonable use of society's property.

Another interesting example is the use of streams and rivers; for example, medieval communities in England had complex rules governing what could be disposed of into streams and rivers, and where and when it could be dumped. Noxious wastes could be disposed of only downstream from the community and at night, when others were unlikely to be drawing water. Anyone abusing these conventions would be sanctioned, by formal fines, by ostracism, or by one of many other ways in which a closed community can express its displeasure with the behavior of one of its members. There are probably similar mechanisms in use today in relatively traditional societies. Such mechanisms work in small, stable societies where everyone knows everyone else and will continue knowing them for most of their lives. In these societies social sanctions count and have force: they are a threat that will limit behavior. But as societies become more mobile and larger, the threat implicit in social sanctions is attenuated. If people expect to change community several times during their lives, then the threat of exclusion from their present community is diminished (Parker 1994).

The other extreme of this spectrum of possible methods of dealing with common property resources is represented by the Conally Hot Oil Act of the United States. This act requires unitized operation of oil fields that overlap several different oil claims. Let's say, for instance, that the government has auctioned off the rights to explore for and develop oil fields on four neighboring areas, all of which have one point in common. There is an oil field centered at this point and extending under all the claims. Clearly this could be an extreme example of a common-pool problem, in the sense that all four claimholders can drill for and extract the oil. And, of course, the more any one claimholder removes, the less there is left for the others. The natural outcome in such a situation is a mad race by the claimholders to remove oil as fast as possible. In many cases this situation has led to the removal of oil far faster than it could be refined or sold and necessitated the construction of aboveground storage facilities. These typically seeped oil, leading to loss, and were a great fire risk.

After many years of losses and fires from this form of field development, the Conally Act required that the claims sharing a common field be merged into one corporate entity, operated as one and owned by the original claimholders. This structure removed the competition between the different oil companies by bringing them all into the same legal corporate entity, so that there were no longer any external effects between them. All oil removed was to be shared by the owners in agreed proportions, removing the conflict of interest. This is an extreme case of the integration examples we have already seen above. Again, it shows that changing organizational boundaries can resolve inefficiencies in the way an economy operates. It is also an interesting example of a noneconomic solution to the common-pool problem.

Let's again turn to commercial fishing, which perhaps provides the most egregious examples of the misuse of common-pool resources. To give some sense of the problem's scale, the fish biomass of several important intensively exploited fisheries, including those of the North Sea, Newfoundland, and Iceland, is now estimated to be only one-tenth of its preexploitation level. Ninety percent of the initial stocks of these fish has been destroyed. From a management perspective there are two different types of fisheries: those lying in the economic zones of coastal nations and therefore, in principle, at least, susceptible to management by these nations, and those on the high seas involving fish that spend much of their lives away from the coasts. These latter are, of course, far harder to manage, as they are beyond the jurisdiction of any nation. Whales operate within this environment, as do tuna, swordfish, marlin, and other large predatory fish as well as migratory salmon. As noted earlier, the fisheries under the control of coastal states are in principle far easier to manage because there is an authority with the legal power to control access and regulate catch, something missing in the other case. The economic measures required to manage these fisheries so that they are used efficiently and without harmful external effects are clear. A good solution, though not the only one, would involve three steps:

1. Determine the level of catch consistent with the survival of the fishery.
2. Next, pass legislation establishing a tradable fishing permit regime for the fishery. Permits would convey the right to catch a certain quantity. Fishing without a permit would be subject to severe penalties. Permits would have to be presented when the catch is sold.
3. Establish a market in fishing permits.

Several beneficial consequences would follow from this system. First and most important, the catch would be limited to a sustainable level. Second, there would be an incentive to take boats out of many of the world's fishing fleets. This is important in many fisheries because the fishing capacity of the fleet is in excess of what is sustainable; reducing the size of the fleet will stabilize the fishing effort at a level consistent with the population's survival. The incentive to retire boats comes from the marketability of the permits.

There are many possible ways of allocating permits: one would be to issue them in proportion to existing catch; another would be to auction them to the highest bidders. If permits were allocated according to previous catch, then all active boats would receive some permits, and the incentive to retire boats would result because retiring a boat would free its permits for sale. In effect, the permits constitute a cash payment for retiring the boat equal to the market value of its permits. If, however, permits are auctioned, then it is necessary to incur a new cost for a boat to continue fishing, the cost of buying its permits. The need to meet this cost will force boatowners to evaluate carefully the value of keeping their boats in operation. It is an incentive to retire the boats—actually, a disincentive—but again, its presence means there is a financial reward in retiring the boat, in the form of avoidance of a cost.

Clearly the catch quota should be set at a level compatible with the survival of the fishery. There certainly can be situations where the right catch level is zero, at least until the stock has recovered from a period of overfishing and reached a sustainable level. A freeze of this type may not only be necessary from a conservation perspective but may also be commercially beneficial and increase the total value of catch over the long run (Dasgupta and Heal 1979). These measures will in general help sustain the population and also improve the profitability of the fishing fleet, which, after all, can only go bankrupt if the fishery collapses. And there are clear instances where overfishing has driven fisheries to collapse and the fishing fleets to bankruptcy. Fishing fleets and fisheries are interdependent: the former cannot survive without the latter. In ecological terms they are symbiotic. Yet fishermen must almost always be persuaded of their own economic self-interest; it is difficult to understand the dynamics or the rationale of this attitude.

What are the options with respect to noncoastal fisheries? Economically they are much the same because the issues are identical. The extra complications are more political and organizational than economic. The problem now is that there is no authority that can regulate the use of these fisheries and, for example, enforce a tradable permit system. Of course this could be established. The Kyoto Protocol is attempting a far more ambitious task, and indeed the Montreal Protocol[1] has achieved something as ambitious, although in a rather different area—regulation of chlorofluorocarbons (CFCs), substances formerly used in refrigerators and air conditioners and found to deplete the ozone layer. The International Whaling Commission took on, and in essence succeeded with, a similar challenge, though it was helped by the charisma and popular appeal associated with whales. If similar public concern were voiced about open-sea fisheries, finding economic structures that would support their efficient use would certainly be possible.

In the case of tuna, there is a management regime in place currently, although it is weakly administered. It assigns an annual catch to each of three regions of the oceans, divides the rights to each region among the nations that have traditionally fished there, and makes catching tuna conditional on having a (nontradable) permit.

---

1. For a detailed history of the negotiations leading to this agreement and a description of the protocol, see Benedick 1998.

In the North American region this policy is enforced relatively strictly by the U.S. Fish and Wildlife Service with assistance from the U.S. Coast Guard, who randomly check fishing boats to monitor their compliance. In other regions, particularly those around Europe, enforcement is much more lax. A major problem here is the Japanese demand for bluefin tuna, which is so great that a single fish may sell for as much as $80,000 to $100,000 in the Tokyo fish market. With prices like these, the incentives to evade regulations are immense. A consequence is the rapid depletion of the stock of bluefin tuna, to the point where its viability may be threatened. Populations of marlin and swordfish, which are similar in many respects to tuna in their ranges and breeding habits, have already collapsed as a result of overfishing.

So far we have thought of fisheries strictly as a source of catch. This is analogous to thinking of forests as only a source of timber, and not asking whether they sequester carbon, purify water, control stream flow, or provide recreational services. Thinking of a forest as a source of timber is like thinking of a historical building as a source of bricks.[2] We may be making the same mistake in thinking of fisheries as a source of protein only. Regrettably, however, we just don't know enough about marine ecosystems to understand what consequences will follow from the extinction of the large predatory fish. Given the existence of extensive interdependencies between species, the consequences could be quite unexpected and possibly harmful.

Taxes and Tradable Permits

So far this chapter has discussed organizational reforms and the management of common-pool resources. Two other market-oriented approaches to managing humanity's impact on its environment are taxes and permit markets. Indeed, they are the two classical approaches to the problem of external effects discussed in Chapter 2. Both operate by closing the gap between the private and social costs of an activity. There are, however, important differences. Permit markets give us an assurance about the level at which the permitted activity will be carried out. In the case of permits for the emission of

---

2. The observation is by Graciela Chichilnisky.

sulfur dioxide in the United States, for example, the Environmental Protection Agency knows that if it issues permits for the emission of X thousand tons of sulfur annually, then this is the amount that will be emitted. What it does not know in advance is the cost of this regulation to the companies affected. This cost is, of course, the permit price and is not known until the market price of permits is established—although it may be guessed on the basis of past experience. With taxes the situation is exactly the opposite. If sulfur emission were to be regulated by taxation, then the cost to affected firms would be the tax rate and would therefore be known in advance. What would not be known in this case is the impact that the tax would have on the level of emissions: only by trial and error would the regulatory agency come to know whether a given tax level would lead to a 5 percent or a 50 percent cutback in emissions. So taxes have merit if we worry most about the cost of the policy that we are about to implement, and permits have merit if our main concern is the extent to which the policy will limit the offending activity.

Either of these approaches—taxes or tradable permits—can be used as a way of regulating human impacts on the planet's main systems. Taxes on the impacting activities will make these less attractive and reduce their extent; this is the idea behind the concept of a carbon tax as a way of reducing greenhouse gas emissions. Alternatively, we can regulate the activities that affect planetary systems by setting a total level that we believe to be acceptable, issuing rights to carry out the activity, and then allowing people to bid on them—the same framework chosen by the parties to the Kyoto Protocol.

This is an appropriate point to discuss in more detail the operations of a tradable permit market (as opposed to the way this market creates incentives for conservation). We will do so in the context of markets for the right to emit greenhouse gases, because this example is so central to the theme of this book. The principles are the same in other contexts.

The composition of the atmosphere, as noted earlier, is a public good, or rather its opposite, a public bad: if the concentration of CO_2 rises for one person or region, then it rises for all. Changes in CO_2 concentration occur primarily because of external effects associated with the use of fossil fuels. The private costs of burning fossil fuels are less than the social costs because of the greenhouse gases they produce. So we want to do two things: one is to bring private and social costs into line, and the other is to provide the desired amount of the public good or bad. Because the atmospheric composition is a public good that is produced by many different agents, aligning private and social costs and benefits is necessary but not sufficient for producing the desired amount of greenhouse gas—or, more to the point, choosing the desired amount of abatement.

The principal features of a greenhouse gas permit regime are as follows:

1. A target level for the total emissions of greenhouse gases is chosen. At Kyoto this was based on the 1990 emission levels and has to be attained by the year 2004.
2. Permits to emit greenhouse gases up to this total are issued to participating countries. These can be traded between them in a market.
3. Next, the permits are allocated to participating countries according to a rule chosen by them. This is a very controversial stage because the permits will have great market value. At this stage the participating countries are in effect distributing new wealth created by the privatization of the right to use the atmosphere for disposing of CO_2.

This system achieves two main goals. First, it fixes the emissions of CO_2 by participating countries at the level of the total number of permits issued, thus bringing the fundamental problem under control. Second, it raises the total cost of greenhouse gas emissions by the market price of a permit, providing companies with an incentive to reduce emissions.

Note that even if a company has all the permits that it needs, it still has an incentive to reduce emissions. The point is that the company faces an opportunity cost of polluting: if it were to cut back pollution, it would need fewer permits and could sell the surplus. So even clean firms have an incentive to be cleaner.

Because of the second point, there is an incentive to keep looking for cleaner technologies. This is different from a regulatory regime that stipulates a maximum emission of greenhouse gases, because under that regime, once a company meets the target it has no incentive to do better. It has been used so far for the regulation of vehicle emissions: regulators have specified maximum acceptable levels and in some cases even specified how the levels should be attained. Such an approach clearly kills all incentive to innovate. The effect of permit markets on innovation has been very clear in the market for sulfur emission permits in the United States. Initially (in the early 1990s) in that market, the price of permits was about $1,000 per ton of sulfur, and the expectation was that it would rise. Now it is under $100 per ton and falling. One of the reasons for this remarkable drop is that this regime has provided continuous stimulus to the development and introduction of new cleaner technologies (Kerr 1998).

In the case of greenhouse gas emission markets, undoubtedly the most difficult point is reaching agreement on the allocation of emission rights between countries. Chapter 5 discussed this issue in the context of carbon sequestration. If we issue permits to emit, say, 4 billion tons of carbon per year, each potentially worth $20 per ton, then we are issuing money to a total value of $80 billion. Naturally every country wants a bigger rather than a smaller share of it, so that countries favor allocation rules that benefit them and those like them. In particular, developing countries hope that they may benefit from the newly created wealth and that it may be used to redress some of the gross inequalities in international income levels. Probably many of you reading this book spend more on your domestic pets each year than the income levels of hundreds of millions of the Earth's human inhabitants, and it is natural to seek any opportunity to redress this type of inequality. In fact, there are economic reasons for thinking that an allocation of emission permits that favors the poorer countries is not only fairer but also more conducive to efficiency than one favoring rich countries. Efficiency here is used in the sense of Pareto efficiency, discussed in Chapter 2. Why would this be so?

Note first that allocating more emission permits to the poorer countries is equivalent to requiring that they shoulder less of the burden of abating greenhouse gases. Possession of permits, of course, is equivalent to not having to abate—although, as noted above, there is always an incentive to abate because of the market value of the permits. Why is it possibly more efficient that less of the abatement burden be placed on poorer countries? There is some evidence that the productivity of investment is higher in developing countries than in the industrial ones (Chichilnisky 2000). Because one of the consequences of increased abatement may be a reduction in the funds available for investment in new factories, the cost of abatement will be lower wherever the productivity of the investment foregone is least. If this productivity is lower in richer countries, then the cost of abatement will be lower there. And efficiency requires that we seek to abate emissions wherever the costs are lowest.

This argument runs counter to arguments that have been made in the context of emissions trading, which claim that the costs of abatement are lower in developing countries, so that it is rational for these countries to bear a large share of the abatement burden and be paid to do so by the industrial countries. There are two reasons for this apparent contradiction. One is that developing countries have abatement opportunities not available to the industrial countries, such as carbon sequestration in tropical forests, as discussed in Chapter 5. For this reason they can play a role in carbon sequestration that is relatively unique. The second reason is that there are differences in the concept of cost. It may be true that abatement through changes in industrial processes will cost, say, $5 per ton in India and $10 per ton in the United States, so that it is apparently less costly in India. However, $5 in India is probably worth far more than $10 in the United States, where average income levels are many times higher. "Worth more" means that $5 saved in India will lead to a far greater increase in social well-being than $10 saved in the United States. So the cost of abatement in terms of human welfare may nevertheless be greater in India than in the United States. Straight cost comparisons in terms of current dollars do not capture this point

There is another reason that a distribution biased toward the poorer countries may be helpful in reaching efficiency: in a permit market controlling the production of a public good, economic efficiency requires that all countries should choose similar trade-offs between climate stabilization and consumption. They must all be willing to give up similar amounts of private consumption to promote the public good of climate stability. Reducing disparities in income levels will reduce differences in these tradeoffs because they depend upon the level of affluence.[3]

Public Goods

The topic of permit markets leads naturally to a more general discussion of policies toward the provision of public goods. These are particularly relevant in the environmental context because, as noted previously, so many environmental services are public goods. They are also privately produced public goods—that is, the production of environmental services is the outcome of millions or even billions of separate decisions about energy use or land use. Traditionally, public goods have been goods that are appropriately produced by a central authority—goods such as law and order, defense, and public health. They have mainly been the responsibility of the public sector, hence the term *public goods*. Because environmental public goods are privately produced, there are more problems to solve with them than with traditional public goods. We have to decide

- how much should be produced,
- who will pay for this production, and
- who should carry out the production.

Only the first two items apply to services such as law and order and defense, and these questions have traditionally been answered by the political process. Political parties have proposed different levels of production of public goods and different ways of distributing the financial burden of providing them, and the electorate has chosen between them. When a choice is made, a public-sector entity carries out the production and the government administers the chosen distribution of the costs through the tax system. The market sector of the economy has been involved at most marginally in the provision of traditional public goods; they have been the concern of the public and nonmarket sector.

With environmental public goods the issues are more complex. Because so many individuals and businesses are involved in their pro-

---

3. For details, see Chichilnisky and Heal 2000.

duction, the government cannot manage their output. The market has to be involved. This is why we are increasingly seeking to manage atmospheric and other forms of pollution through the use of permit markets, as in the cases of sulfur dioxide and greenhouse gases. But, as noted in Chapter 2, markets and public goods do not normally mix well, because appropriating the benefits from the provision of a public good is problematic. Such goods are by definition "nonexcludable," meaning that those who provide them cannot easily appropriate the social benefits from their acts. So naturally they will underprovide public goods.

There is one way of circumventing this problem, which is to use what economists call *Lindahl markets*. These are markets in which there may be many different prices for the same good.[4] In such a market you and I may pay different prices for the same good or service. The price paid for a permit in such markets could depend on some characteristic of the buyer, such as his or her nationality. This is not normal in markets for private goods, although it certainly does happen. Perhaps the best example is the market for airline tickets. A ticket from London to New York may sell for many different prices, depending on how far ahead it is bought, whether the buyer stays over a Saturday night, and other factors. The Web sites of United Airlines and American Airlines show up to twenty different fares on popular routes such as New York to Los Angeles. What is happening here is that the airlines are trying to charge different people different prices for the same service, because some consumers are willing to pay more than others. Typically business travelers are willing to pay more than vacationers, and in response the airlines seek pricing policies that allow them to take advantage of that. Economists call this "price discrimination." Auto companies also practice price discrimination, in this case by country. For instance, in Europe, different prices are charged for the same cars in different countries.

The same type of practice is needed in markets for public goods if they are to attain efficient outcomes. A complete explanation is too complex to introduce here. The main point is that in the market, each participant must contribute to the financing of the public good

---

4. For details, see Foley 1970.

an amount equal to the value that he or she places on it, which will typically differ from person to person or group to group. There is a difference: in the case of public goods this practice can be justified on the grounds of its social utility, which is not true in the case of car sales.

This is a problem, because the permit markets introduced so far are like markets for regular private goods; they have uniform prices that are the same for all traders. If we present all traders in these markets with the same prices, then for efficient outcomes we need to distribute the emission permits in relatively egalitarian ways, as discussed above. So while the permit markets we are using to date are a great improvement on any other alternatives so far considered, they are too simple in structure to capture fully the conditions needed for efficient provision of environmental public goods. We may ultimately migrate to a system in which the prices in these markets are country-specific.

Regulation

Many important elements of environmental policy do not conform to any of the approaches discussed in this book. For example, gasoline emissions are regulated by specific laws governing the use of particular techniques for restricting emissions. Endangered species in the United States are protected by the Endangered Species Act (ESA),[5] and internationally the equivalent is the Convention on International Trade in Endangered Species (CITES). Both the ESA and CITES work by specifically prohibiting certain actions, rather than through the economic mechanisms outlined in these chapters, as does the regulation of vehicle emissions. In general, such approaches increase the costs of compliance with the regulation considerably.

Take the case of vehicle emissions. Suppose that vehicle manufacturers had certain emission allowances for their average vehicles or had an aggregate allowance for their annual sales as a whole. Suppose in addition that they could trade allowances with other manufacturers, so that if Ford is below its target emissions and General

---

5. For a more detailed analysis of the Endangered Species Act, see Brown and Shogren 1998.

Motors over, then Ford could sell its surplus to General Motors. This would give Ford an incentive to continue reducing emissions even when it has reached its emission target. And it would reduce costs at General Motors. Everyone would gain from this kind of modification of "command-and-control" regulations. The British Petroleum Amoco oil group has recently begun using such a system internally. It intends to reduce group emissions of carbon dioxide and methane to 10 percent below their 1990 levels by 2010 and will do this by establishing an in-group trading mechanism rather than through regulation of emissions.

Some approaches to modifying the ESA are based on these ideas. Many landowners greatly dislike the ESA as it can lead to tight restrictions on what they can do with their land if an endangered species is discovered on it. As a result, there have been several local moves to modify its impact and to introduce economic incentives into its operation. A good example is an agreement reached between International Paper and the U.S. Fish and Wildlife Service concerning the red-cockaded woodpecker, *Picoides borealis*. This bird is endangered and nests in forests owned by International Paper. They and the Fish and Wildlife Service agree on a target number of breeding woodpecker pairs, and provided that this number is attained or exceeded, International Paper will be regarded as complying with the ESA, whatever use it makes of the land. Further, the agreement also provides that any surplus can be "banked"—that is, used by the company to offset ESA requirements with respect to red-cockaded woodpeckers elsewhere. It is also possible that title to it could be sold to other landowners and used by them to gain some measure of exemption (Jorling 1999). This ability to store or sell the surplus over the amount required by regulations is called *mitigation banking*. The important point here is that the agreement has reduced the costs of compliance with the ESA without reducing the ESA's effectiveness. Indeed, the benefits go beyond this: as the production of nesting pairs over a target is salable, International Paper now actually has an economic incentive to encourage the endangered species, something it never had with a strict interpretation of the ESA. International Paper currently believes that it can sell banked breeding pairs for about $100,000 each. If several pairs can nest on each acre, this means that the value of land for breeding woodpeckers is greatly in excess of its value as a source of timber. The point of this example is that regulation pure and simple is rarely the best way to go about attaining a conservation goal. The costs of compliance, and therefore the political opposition, can often be greatly reduced by introducing an element of economic incentives. Incentives allow people and institutions to benefit from compliance, which will often improve the effectiveness of the regulation.

A very similar approach is being used under the Clean Water Act, which provides for the conservation of wetlands because of their role in removing impurities from water flowing through them. Companies that want to develop land that is currently a wetland can obtain permission to do so in some states if they provide an equivalent amount of new wetland elsewhere or if they purchase wetland for conservation from a wetlands mitigation bank. Analytically, mitigation banking in either of these cases is similar to a tradable permit system. The key feature of a mitigation banking system is that a regulatory authority establishes a target level for some attribute of the environment that has to be conserved—for example, a target number of breeding pairs of woodpeckers or a target acreage of wetlands. Individual landowners are then given their own targets specifying what they must contribute to the total social target. In making their contribution they are free to go over the target prescribed for them and sell the surplus or to fall short of the target and buy the shortfall from those who have gone over their targets. This is exactly the mechanism used in the case of tradable permits. In effect, the Fish and Wildlife Service has introduced markets in tradable woodpecker permits and tradable wetland permits. In so doing they have greatly improved the operation of the Endangered Species Act and the Clean Water Act.

This illustrates a more general but closely related point mentioned several times before. Regulation operates by telling people what they must and must not do. It represents a negative approach to attaining conservation goals. In general, we will be more successful in attaining our goals if we make it in people's interests to attain them rather than forcing them to behave in ways conducive to conservation. We need to use the carrot as well as the stick, and ideally much more than the stick. Approaches such as permit markets and taxes operate by presenting people with incentives that make it in their interests to attain conservation goals.

Buying Public Goods

There are, of course, many other carrots that society could offer to induce people to make choices that are conservative with respect to the environment. We could simply pay them to make the right choices. In effect, we could make society the buyer of the public goods provided by environmentally conservative choices. This way, we could overcome the free-rider problem that bedevils the provision of public goods. There is an economic cost to such policies, which is that if society is to pay for public goods, it has to raise the revenue to do this in some way, perhaps by taxation or by running public enterprises more profitably than otherwise. However, in some cases, this cost may be well worth paying, and indeed there may be cases in which there is no extra cost in providing economic incentives for supplying environmental public goods.

Consider as an example the area of agricultural policy. Agricultural practices have a profound impact on environmental systems, such as the effects of fertilizer use on the nitrogen cycle. It is therefore very important to seek ways of making agricultural practices more environmentally friendly. The agricultural sector is one in which there is already extensive government intervention, usually in the form of programs intended to support the incomes of the farming community. In most industrial countries these programs are widespread and impose substantial costs on the average taxpayer. They have proven remarkably resilient politically, having survived many attempts to cut them back. In the European Community (EU), support to the agricultural sector is provided through the Common Agricultural Policy (CAP), which governs payments to farmers to compensate for low prices or poor yields. By supporting the prices of foods artificially this policy has led to production greatly in excess of the needs of the European Community, at costs that make it uneconomic to sell the surpluses on world markets, where prices are lower than in Europe and lower even than European production costs. The CAP has thus achieved the twin goals of producing unwanted food and encouraging farmers to damage the environment.

At last the EU is seriously considering reforming its agricultural policy. One of the options is to stop paying farmers for producing unwanted food and instead pay them to manage their land according to ecologically sound principles. A recent editorial in the *Financial Times* (1998) suggested exactly this: "We want the countryside as a thing of beauty and ecological sustenance, in which food may or may not play a part." The writer went on to suggest that farmers earn their living "not by tonnage of output, but by footage of hedgerows or dry-stone walls, or by acreage of wild flowers."

A similar system is already in operation on a trial basis in part of Wales.[6] Rather than subsidizing the production of food, this scheme pays for the installation and preservation of hedgerows, wetlands, copses, saltmarshes, uncropped field margins, broad-leaved woodland, and other features of the original landscape that are supportive of biodiversity. The political point behind the Welsh system and the suggestion of the *Financial Times* writer is that there are strong pressures to subsidize the living standards of the agricultural community: this seems to be something to which many industrial societies are committed. Given this political fact, European and American governments need to find formats for the subsidy that are environmentally positive rather than harmful. They need ways of doing this that avoid the waste inherent in producing and then destroying food that is not needed and doing so in environmentally destructive ways. If what we want of the countryside is that it should be close to natural ecosystems and a place of beauty for recreation, then the natural implication is that we should pay farmers to provide precisely that. In effect, we would then be establishing a market in ecosystem services, with the public sector the buyer. Because through our roles as taxpayers we are already subsidizing the agricultural sector exten-

---

6. Administered by the Countryside Council for Wales, this scheme in known as Tir Cymen. See www.ccw.gov.uk for more details.

sively, the extra cost would be zero: this is a redeployment of existing funds to attain a socially preferable outcome.

Similar ideas are in operation in U.S. agricultural policies. The Conservation Reserve Program of the U.S. Department of Agriculture (USDA) pays farmers to take environmentally sensitive land out of production and establish a form of land cover that will conserve it. Under this program, introduced as a part of the 1985 Food Security Act, farmers offer the USDA land that they are willing to remove from production. They also indicate a rent that they require be paid to keep the land out of production. The USDA then ranks these offers according to an Environmental Benefits Index (EBI), which takes into account the extent to which the land offered provides wildlife habitat, the potential for erosion, and air- and water-quality benefits from reduced erosion. The requested rent also plays a role in the ranking of the offers.[7] Currently, over 30 million acres are being held out of production in this program, slightly over 10 percent of U.S. cropland. The United States also has a Wetlands Reserve,[8] which is funded to buy wetland from farmers or to pay farmers to conserve them as wetland rather than converting them to agricultural uses. In addition, the Swampbuster provisions of the 1985 Food Security Act state that no federal agricultural subsidies or supports can be received by a farmer in any year in which he or she has planted crops on a converted wetland. This is a serious sanction and has probably deterred many from wetland conversion.

The same idea—payment by society for the preservation of natural systems—can be applied in many other areas. However, in general, it makes most sense politically where the services are provided on a local level and the paying community receives a clear benefit from the services that they are purchasing. Something very close to this is also in operation in Costa Rica, where national parks are paid for some of the ecosystem services that they provide to local communities: watershed and flood-control services, pollination services, and, in one case, even waste disposal services. Again, the public purse is buying environmental public goods from their providers,

---

7. For details, see U.S. Department of Agriculture 1997.

8. Ibid.

and in so doing it is producing incentives for the conservation of the underlying ecosystems.

National Income

Finally, a rather different kind of policy observation: fundamental to many of the problems in how we interact with our environment is our failure to understand the importance of environmental services to our society. Chapter 1 developed this point. We would make progress toward correcting this deficiency if we recorded and measured economic performance and progress in a way that records the contribution of the natural environment to the economy and also records our impact on its potential to continue providing services into the future. Currently our main measure of economic progress and economic performance is national income. What would work more effectively is a revision of how national income is measured so that it reflects better the economic contributions made by natural ecosystems and the impact of our activities on them. A country's national income is measured as the sum of the value added in every business in the country. *Value added* is the difference between the value of inputs purchased and the value of output sold. *National income* is the sum of this number for all enterprises in the economy, with some rather arbitrary corrections for the activities of not-for-profit entities such as government agencies, hospitals, and educational institutions. The value of the services provided by these institutions is taken to be the cost of providing them. Under certain rather idealized conditions, changes in national income give a good indication of changes in the well-being of members of society. Unfortunately, this concept does not work well in the context of environmental impacts.

One example will suffice to make this point clear. Suppose that in the case of the New York City watershed discussed in Chapter 3, the city had permitted residential development of the Catskills and built a filtration plant to purify its water supply in place of the region's natural purification processes. We have seen plenty of evidence that this would have been the wrong decision. Yet this option would have led to a much larger increase in national income than the decision to conserve. National income would have increased because of the activities of the construction companies in the Catskills, and it would have increased further because of the activities of the companies building the filtration plant. So there would have been two sources of increase in national income: the destruction of natural ecosystems, and the construction of replacements for them. Conservation, by contrast, led to no increase in national income. Clearly we are measuring something wrongly.

There are two basic errors in the way we currently go about measuring national income. One is that we do not record the value of the services that we get from the environment as a part of society's well-being. The other is that we do not record the depreciation of our environmental assets. The first of these points should be quite clear, given the discussions in earlier chapters on the importance of the services that our societies obtain from natural ecosystems. They make important contributions to our standard of living, and we are underestimating national income if we omit them. If we compare two societies that are identical in all respects except for the integrity of their natural ecosystems, then national income will appear to be identical and we will be led to assume that both are equally well-off. Yet in fact the society with the more intact ecosystems—the purer water and cleaner environment—will have the higher living standards in most people's judgments.

The second point is also rather easy to understand. Natural ecosystems are assets to the societies in which they function. An asset is understood by economists as something that can provide a flow of services over time. Houses, cars, factories, and computers are all assets because they can provide a flow of services over time. And intuitively we all know that we should allow for the depreciation of our assets. Certainly all businesses allow for this in their accounting procedures—the law requires them to if they are public companies, because to do otherwise would mislead the investing public. Companies therefore subtract the depreciation of their assets from their earnings in computing their profits, which are the normal measure of corporate performance. To the extent that a country reduces the value of its environmental assets—and these are assets that provide important services—it should also deduct the depreciation of those assets from its national income. To do otherwise would be like a company generating profits by selling its assets and not revealing it has done so in its annual report. In fact, in the United States, oil companies are required to show the depletion of their oil reserves as a cost to be subtracted from their profits. At the national level there is no equivalent requirement.

Let's return to the New York City example to see how these two changes—incorporating the value of environmental services and allowing for the depreciation of environmental assets—would change matters. First, the destruction of the Catskills watershed would lead to a drop in national income as the value of the services derived from this source declined. This would be recorded as the provision of less potable, and hence less valuable, water by the watershed. Second, it would also reduce national income because the destruction of a valuable asset would be matched by a corresponding depreciation term in the national income calculation: we would subtract from national income the loss of value of the watershed, just as a corporation subtracts loss of value of plant and equipment.

If the development of the Catskills was in fact a bad decision, then these two terms—the drop in value of the water from the watershed and the loss of value of the watershed itself—would more than offset the additions to national income resulting from the development in the Catskills and the construction of a filtration plant. National income would decline as a result of the bad decision, reflecting the fact that this decision made society worse off. Current national income is a seriously misleading measure; there is little doubt that at least in the United States, corporations publishing income figures that are misleading as measures of national income currently published by government would be sued by their shareholders and reprimanded by the Securities and Exchange Commission.

Summary

This chapter has reviewed a range of policy measures that can act as alternatives to, or can supplement, the use of markets to provide the incentives needed to conserve valuable ecosystems. They include changes in organization, property rights, the use of taxes and permits, and certain types of regulation. Fisheries and agriculture—two of the oldest human activities—provide some of the most challenging areas for applying these ideas.

Chapter 9

Sustainability

If a man takes no thought about what is distant,
he will find sorrow near at hand.

—Confucius

Can existing patterns of human activity safely continue unaltered
over the long term, or will they lead to unacceptable consequences?
This is a concise statement of the central issue underlying discussions
of sustainability. It is closely related to the concerns of the previous
chapters; indeed, to some degree this entire book so far has touched
on the issue of sustainability without explicitly using the word. That
was quite deliberate: *sustainability* means many things, not all consistent, so that discussions about it have not always been illuminat-
ing.[1] However, many of the concerns prompting an interest in sustainability are precisely those discussed so far: possible climate
change, the loss of biodiversity, and, in general, human impacts on
important biogeochemical cycles and ecosystems. These impacts suggest that a continuation of present trends will lead to serious damage
to the natural infrastructures of human societies, with negative consequences for human welfare. In short, they suggest that human

---

1. For more details on this discussion and on various interpretations of it, see
Heal 1998.

165

impacts on the biosphere cannot and should not be continued and are unsustainable.

Most natural ecosystems are sustainable: they are driven by an inflow of solar energy and its conversion to biomass, and they could continue their operation indefinitely if these parameters remained unaltered. There is no net accumulation of waste (because of the decomposers and scavengers that are a part of any ecosystem) and no net depletion of nonrenewable resources. Possibly some human societies have operated comparably. Medieval Europe, for example, was surely much closer to this pattern than we are today. It relied on renewable energy (wind, biomass, animal power) and practiced a relatively benign form of agriculture. Traditional farming methods were probably significantly more sustainable than many of our current practices. Population was also rather constant for a long period. (This is not, of course, to suggest that it was an attractive society; clearly in many respects it was not.) A dramatic shift from such a sustainable configuration occurred with the development of technologies based on fossil fuels, namely coal-fired steam engines, which permitted a qualitative change in the scale of the human enterprise and its impact on the natural world and set us firmly on the road to the present.

Suppose we were to adopt the policies of earlier chapters and establish markets in such ecosystem services as carbon sequestration and water management, so that the private and social costs of economic activities would become more equal and the providers of public goods would be able to appropriate the full social returns on them. This is a very tall order, of course. But would we then have a sustainable relationship between the economy and the biosphere?

Unfortunately not. Certainly we would improve matters greatly, but we could still not be sure that our relationship with our natural surroundings was sustainable in the sense set out above. The reason lies in matters of timing. The private and social costs and benefits of actions and policies may occur now; they may also occur far into the future. In fact, for many environmental conservation policies, the costs are incurred now and borne in the near future, yet the benefits will be felt slowly and far into the distant future. Think of conserving a forest: the present generation bears a cost, which is the income lost by not logging. The benefits accrue mainly to future generations as the forest continues to sequester carbon, support biodiversity, and manage water flows and purification. Only a short part of this long stream of benefits helps the present generation. Most conventional economic decision-making algorithms do not place equal weight on costs or benefits now and in the far future. In effect, there is a divergence between the time scales of economic decisions and those of ecological and environmental processes. The result is that this divergence can bias economic choices against sustainability.

Sustainability is above all about what happens in the long term. It is about whether we can continue "indefinitely" as we are, and whether the economic rules of the game lead us to make choices that from an ecological perspective and the perspective of the Earth's life-support systems are viable in the long term. Here "the long term" denotes a period much longer than that normally considered in economic analyses. It denotes a period typically of at least half a century and sometimes as long as several centuries, because this is the type of timescale over which many ecological processes evolve. This is the timescale of climate change and of changes in other major biogeochemical cycles. By contrast, in normal corporate decisions, five years is considered a very long time. Indeed, from many perspectives, it is. In the computer industry five years is long enough for a company to be founded, rise to prominence in a field, and be valued at billions of dollars. It is long enough for technologies to change almost totally. Probably the longest time horizons ever considered in economic decisions are those involved in infrastructure choices—choices about roads, bridges, airports, sewage systems, and water supply systems. Even for these, thirty years is considered a long time. So there is a problem in reconciling the traditional economic approach to time and the typical economic timescale with that required if we are to come to grips with sustainability.

Discounting and Valuing the Future

Environmental assets provide flows of services over very long periods of time. New York's Catskills watershed has purified water and controlled stream flow for hundreds—if not thousands—of years, and if left intact will continue to do so for at least as long again.

Insects have been pollinating plants for much, much longer and could continue as long again if not driven extinct by pesticides (Nabhan and Buchmann 1997). No human systems have such lifespans. Knowledge and culture are the only assets we produce that can rival natural assets in their durability: Shakespeare thrives at half a millennium, Plato and Pythagoras at several millennia. Because of the totally different time scales of the capital assets that humans and nature produce, the techniques that we use for valuing human-made capital assets really cannot be applied to natural assets.

We assign a dollar value to the capital that we produce by means of cost-benefit analysis. In this we take as the benefits of capital the present discounted value of the flow of services that it produces. *Discounting* means giving less weight to the future than to the present. As noted in Chapter 7, the rationalization for this procedure is that money earns interest when invested, so that $100 invested today at a rate of 5 percent will be worth $105 one year hence. It follows that $105 a year hence is equivalent to—that is, has a present value of—$100 today. At first this may appear to be a compelling and logical estimate of future value. However, by discounting we in effect choose an implicit time horizon, a date beyond which nothing matters. As shown in Figure 9.1, this is in the region of twenty to thirty years: at a 5 percent discount rate, one dollar twenty years hence has a present value of 22 cents and at 10 percent its value is 5 cents.[2] We are in effect giving little or no weight to benefits that occur more than a quarter of a century ahead.

When we apply this kind of calculation to environmental assets, we are ignoring most of the benefits that they will provide to human societies; we are accounting for just twenty years of the benefits that these assets contribute when they could contribute, at no extra cost, for twenty decades or perhaps twenty centuries. Clearly we are undervaluing them grossly.

The normal method of ranking development paths and investment projects, including environmental conservation projects, is by the present discounted value of net benefits. That is, alternatives are ranked by the present discounted value of benefits minus that of costs. Many authors have expressed reservations about the balance

---

2. $e^{-0.05 \times 20} = 0.22$ and $e^{-0.1 \times 20} = 0.05$.

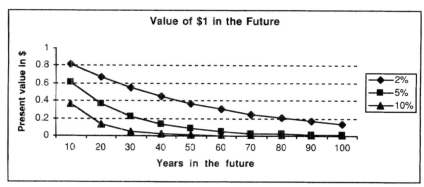

FIGURE 9.1. Value of $1 at future dates up to one hundred years.

that this method strikes between present and future.[3] The reason, as noted already, is that a positive discount rate forces a fundamental asymmetry between the treatments of, and the implicit valuations of, present and future generations, particularly those very far into the future. This asymmetry in the treatment of present and future is especially troubling with environmental matters such as climate change, species extinction, and disposal of nuclear waste, as many of their consequences may be felt only in the very long run indeed, a hundred or more years into the future. At any positive discount rate these consequences will clearly not loom large, or even at all, in project evaluations.

Although discounting would discourage long-term investments in ecological infrastructure, societies obviously are in fact worried about these issues and are actively considering devoting substantial resources to them. To accomplish this, economic institutions and procedures should reflect better our values and concerns, so we have to find an alternative to the discounting approach.

Interestingly, there is empirical evidence (see Lowenstein and Elster 1992) that individuals making their own decisions do not in fact compare present and future by discounting the future relative to the present at a constant discount rate, as in the standard approach. Rather, they seem to apply a discount rate that varies with the time horizon. The rate is quite high over short periods (15 to 20 percent

3. Cline (1992) and Broome (1992) have argued for the use of a zero discount rate in the context of global warming.

over a few years) but falls rapidly with the length of the horizon under consideration, to as low as 2 percent for horizons of several decades. So as we make long-term decisions—for example, about saving for retirement—we may place more weight on what happens in the future than do governments and corporations.[4]

Discounting has always been a source of controversy between economists and those from other disciplines interested in the environment. Perhaps less well known is the fact that discounting has been a source of controversy within the economics profession. Frank Ramsey, the first person to think seriously about dynamic economics and author of a seminal 1928 article on long-range planning, commented that discounting "is ethically indefensible and arises merely from the weakness of the imagination." His contemporary, Roy Harrod (1948), added that it is a "polite expression for rapacity and the conquest of reason by passion." These are strong words, from people who clearly believe that they are right.[5]

Why has discounting been controversial in economics, and why

---

4. One rationalization for this is that people respond to proportional rather then absolute changes in distance in time. Postponing a reward by one year from the first to the second year and by one year from the twentieth to the twenty-first are both one-year postponements, but one matters a lot and the other doesn't. One is a doubling and the other a 5 percent change. If it is the percentage change that matters and not the number of years, then people discount according to the logarithm of time—thus, $e^{-0.1 \log t}$ for a 10 percent discount rate. This leads to a far higher relative value on the future. For example, after one hundred years, discounting logarithmically at ten percent gives almost 14,000 times more weight than discounting exponentially. After fifty years, the ratio is 100. Over only ten years, the difference is a factor of 2.

5. It is ironic that a practice so roundly condemned by the founders of intertemporal economics has come to occupy so central a position in the field. It may be fair to say that until now discounted utilitarianism has dominated our approach more because of a lack of convincing alternatives than because of the conviction that it inspires. It has proven particularly controversial with noneconomists concerned with environmental valuations. The legitimacy of discounting is in fact a most complex issue, and the comments of Ramsey and Harrod, though perceptive and pointed, do not do it justice. Discounting of future utilities is in some sense logically necessary: without it one encounters a variety of unsettling paradoxes, as explained in Heal 1998. The distinction between discounting future utilities in the evaluation of development programs and the discounting of future benefits in cost-benefit studies also has to be borne in mind.

has the controversy been particularly acute in the environmental area? The key point about the environmental area is the one that began this chapter. Environmental problems often force one to consider long time horizons. In the climate change area, half a century is a typical timeframe. The same is true about species extinction and biodiversity loss and storage of nuclear waste. Scientific processes relating to the environment naturally unfold over this type of horizon. But, as noted several times, such time horizons are completely outside the normal range in economic decision making (Lowenstein and Elster 1992). Corporations and governments normally look, at the very most, a few decades ahead, rather than centuries. The longest "normal" time horizons in economics are those for infrastructure investments such as power stations, where thirty years is a possible horizon. Five to fifteen years is much more common as a planning horizon and is still longer than the average. Horizons of this type are not long enough to raise one of the issues central to long-term environmental problems, namely equity between generations. For five to fifteen years in the context of business plans, the efficient use of capital is the focal issue. For half a century or more in the context of the planet's life-support systems, equity between generations and "sustainability" naturally come to center stage (although efficient use of capital does not leave the stage). So normal economic problems and long-term environmental problems have quite different timescales and involve different issues. It is natural that the methodology for one does not perfectly fit the other.

In resolving long-term environmental issues, we want to achieve two aims. One is to strike a fair balance between the present and the future; the other is to use our limited economic resources, including capital, efficiently. What is involved in efficient use of capital? It requires that the rates of return on all types of capital and durable goods and equipment (including durable natural systems) are the same. Establishing markets in all such goods or their services will meet this condition.[6] So we should let a market charge for the use of

---

6. In a market context this becomes a no-arbitrage condition. *No arbitrage* means that all assets offer the same rate of return, allowing for differences in the risks associated with them. Competitive asset markets naturally bring about this situation.

capital, which gives rise naturally to a cost of capital. We need a cost for capital to make sure we don't waste it; however green your complexion, you certainly want to use society's capital as productively as possible. However, establishing a market price for the use of capital and discounting the future are two quite different matters. Neither implies the other.[7] To repeat,

> The key social objectives are
> • efficient use of capital and
> • a fair balance between the present and the future.

Establishing markets in the services of capital assets and equalizing rates of return can move us toward the first of these objectives, efficient use of capital assets. How do we strike a proper balance between present and future? This is a harder question to answer, a matter of ethical judgment, the same category of judgment we make when we say that a particular distribution of income within society is acceptable or is too unequal. This does not mean that it is just a matter of opinion and that all opinions are equally good. There are some basic principles that we can establish, and these can provide valuable guides. But in the end, there is no purely scientific definition of a "proper" balance between present and future. The controversy within economics over discounting arises from disagreements about what is a proper balance, plus perhaps some confusion of the issues of intergenerational equity and efficient use of capital and a lack of clarity on how they interact.

What about adopting a more future-friendly decision-making method than exponential discounting? Certainly there are possibilities here.[8] One is to replace the ranking of projects according to the present value of net benefits with a ranking in terms of the level of sustainable net benefits, that is, the level of net benefits that can be continued over a very long period. As noted above, empirical studies seem to suggest that individuals do not follow the standard model

---

7. See, e.g., Dasgupta and Heal 1979, chapter 7. The condition referred to here—equal rates of return—is necessary but not sufficient for efficiency in the use of capital assets of types.

8. They are discussed at length in Heal 1998. An interesting possibility is to be found in Chichilnisky 1996.

when making choices over time. It appears that most individuals use discount rates that are lower the longer the time horizon they are considering.

Where does this leave us with respect to valuing the future, particularly the long-term future? There are ways of valuing income streams over long time periods that give more weight to the future than the standard practice and that are just as compelling and logical—indeed, from many perspectives, even more so. There is nothing particularly sacrosanct logically about the usual way of doing things; equally compelling alternatives are available and will place substantially more weight on the future.

Most of the alternatives are consistent with the competitive market, in the sense that corporations seeking to maximize profits can attain them. However, this may not mean maximizing the present value of profits. Adopting these may mean that corporations have to seek to maximize the long-run level of profits or perhaps some combination of that and the present value of profits. Intuitively this makes sense: fishing fleets are clearly seeking to maximize short-run profits to the detriment of long-run profits, and paying more attention to the latter would lead to quite different behavior. Unfortunately, what it would take to change these behavior patterns throughout most of society is not clear.

Some points are clear, however. Certain types of institutions make it their business to lobby for future-oriented decisions and to try to tip the scales in that direction. These are usually NGOs (nongovernmental organizations). In particular, in the United Kingdom, the National Trust has as its primary purpose the purchase of land and properties of outstanding environmental or historical importance, to be held in trust for the future. The Nature Conservancy in the United States has a similar role vis-à-vis the environment, as does the Trust for Public Lands (TPL). More should be done, but these institutions indicate a potential mechanism for implementing future-oriented decisions even in a society where most decisions involve short time horizons.

Market Forces and Sustainability

An important general point implied by the analysis so far is that this is an area where we cannot expect to rely on market forces without a lot of intervention and assistance. There are no markets for goods and services well into the future, so that with respect to the future the market cannot perform effectively its role of bringing together suppliers and consumers and providing incentives for the former to meet the needs of the latter. There are actually some futures markets, markets for goods to be delivered in the future, but these are for buying and selling specialist financial instruments and commodities and cover only a few years ahead. Even if we had markets for goods fifty years ahead, they would not solve our problem because future generations, the people whose welfare concerns us, would not be available to trade on these markets and vote with their dollars. The markets could therefore not reflect their interests. Market forces do determine current levels of investment, which of course affect future levels of welfare, but they usually do this with reference to short-term considerations. It would be a remarkable coincidence if they were to provide the right incentives to build for the long-run future.

Nevertheless, some generations have endowed their successors generously. The Victorians lavishly endowed subsequent generations with many types of infrastructure; to again cite the New York example, the Victorians built a water distribution system whose capacity greatly exceeded their own needs and that has been adequate until very recently. In doing so, they saved subsequent generations the costs of huge and disruptive investments in under-street water conduits. However, other generations have behaved in quite the opposite fashion—think of our generation with respect to fishing stocks or medieval Britain with respect to forests. Many once-valuable commercial fisheries have been overfished to the point where their value has been destroyed—particularly those in the North Sea, off Iceland, and off Newfoundland. Britain before the Industrial Revolution was heavily forested, but much of this forest cover was destroyed for charcoal burning, iron smelting, and house and ship building. Historians have argued that the Industrial Revolution in Britain and the associated development of steam power, the first technology based on fossil fuel, was motivated by the exhaustion of wood supplies in Britain. It is noteworthy that most of the examples of parsimony with respect to bequests relate to natural resources, and those of generosity relate to manufactured resources.

Sometimes financial constraints can conspire to foreshorten our perspective on the future quite dramatically, even more than is implied by a discount rate in the range of 5 to 10 percent. In some of these cases financial markets can play a positive role in establishing a better balance between present and future.

The best way of appreciating this point is through an example. Suppose that a developing country has valuable environmental assets, such as forests, and can derive some income from these—by carbon sequestration or bioprospecting, for instance. But suppose in addition that this country is very poor and is in a state of economic and financial crisis, in desperate need of income. Many countries meet the assumption of being desperately poor, but unfortunately not the assumption of deriving income from carbon sequestration or biodiversity. Indonesia, for instance, is very poor and in urgent need of income; sadly, it is not yet able to generate income from the services that its unique and extensive biosphere provides to the rest of humanity. Now suppose that our hypothetical country faces a steady stream of income continuing into the future from its environmental assets but has an acute need for income now. It would gladly trade future income for present income. The inability to do this might lead it to choose the strategy of selling forests as timber, which offers lots of cash now and none in the future, rather than conserving them, which gives less cash now but more in total. Here financial markets can help. One of their main purposes is to move income over time and let people and institutions spend now in anticipation of future income. This is exactly what a mortgage does—it lets the borrowers consume in excess of income now in exchange for consuming less than income in the future. If environmental assets could provide income, they could act as securities for loans and mortgages, potentially reducing the pressure to destroy them to raise current income.

In a situation such as the one described, financial institutions or markets could readily provide current income against the security of repayment from future environmental income. To put flesh on these bones, consider the case of Costa Rica and Merck, discussed in

Chapter 6. Costa Rica's InBio signed an agreement with Merck under which it provides Merck with specimens to be tested for pharmaceutical potential, in exchange for a one-time payment and a royalty on any drug eventually produced. The right to a royalty is a right to a part of the profits of specified Merck products. This right could eventually produce huge payments, but not for perhaps twenty or more years in the future—after all, it can take fifteen years to take a drug from conception to market. Costa Rica has here a right to an uncertain future income. Some or all of this right could be sold for cash now; it constitutes a form of security deriving its value from profits on certain Merck products. In fact, it would be a type of share in Merck: regular shares in Merck are legally rights to a fraction of their total profits. If Costa Rica were to suffer from an acute cash crisis, this ability to convert the agreement into cash now would enable it to bring future income forward and avoid pressure to liquidate environmental assets because of cash constraints.

The use of financial markets to anticipate income does not change fundamentally the way we value the future relative to the present. It allows us to avoid situations where current income shortages might force us into shortsighted choices that we will subsequently regret. A current income crisis can push the value of the future into insignificance relative to the present. The ability to anticipate future income can avoid this problem.

Where does this discussion leave us with respect to attaining sustainable ways of using the natural environment? To what extent will implementing the policies suggested in earlier chapters lead to a sustainable mode of operation? The answer seems to be that adopting the policies of the earlier chapters—using markets to provide conservation incentives where possible—is a necessary step in attaining sustainability but is not on its own sufficient. It is a step in the right direction, probably a large step, but will not get us all the way to where we might want to go if sustainability is our overall goal. The policies of earlier chapters will provide incentives for conservation and so will stop some of the current damage to Earth's life-support systems, but they will not necessarily strike what we think of as the right balance between present and future, between our successors and us. For this we need to develop institutions and procedures that are specifically targeted at shifting the balance between the short and long runs and that give consideration to and represent the interests of future generations. We also have to reconsider the procedures by which governments and corporations make decisions that involve trade-offs between the present and the future.

Chapter 10

Summary and Conclusions

This book has presented many ecological and economic concepts, so it is worthwhile to summarize them here.

First, we saw that the environment, in the form of natural ecosystems, planetary biogeochemical cycles, biodiversity, and their interactions, provides essential infrastructure for human societies. Without it, much of our own infrastructure would be built in vain or could not even be built. Without it, it would be difficult, if not impossible, to maintain anything remotely like our present lifestyles. We know of societies that have destroyed their ecological foundations and themselves, and there is compelling evidence that human activity is affecting global systems in a manner unprecedented in planetary history. Environmental conservation has to be seen in this context: it is household maintenance, home repair for our species, global housekeeping, earthkeeping.

An obvious implication is that we need to take this situation seriously. Environmental conservation is not a luxury or a frill. We clearly need policies and institutions that ensure we maintain our global home. These must be largely economic policies and institutions, because it is mainly our economic activity that threatens our planetary home and the infrastructure that it provides. We've discussed some of the basic ideas concerning the operation of a market economy, and in particular the concepts of private and social costs and of public goods. We also looked at the concept of the invisible hand, the tendency of a market economic system to use society's resources efficiently under certain conditions. A market system tends to underprovide public goods and goods whose provision benefits people other than the provider. Correspondingly, it overprovides goods whose social costs exceed their private costs, the classic examples being pollutants.

Understanding some of the basic concepts of market economics is important in clarifying what we can and cannot expect of market prices. In particular, market economics shows clearly that market price and importance to society are not the same; this is the point of the centuries-old diamond-water paradox. From the perspective of conserving important natural ecosystems, this difference is not critical: what we need to establish is incentives for conservation, and this in turn depends on the ability of the owners of the system to appropriate as rewards some of the benefits they convey to others.

Several chapters explored the implications of these ideas for the management of our interactions with the environment. Three types of ecosystems stand out as candidates for management by the market: watersheds (Chapter 3), areas attracting ecotourism (Chapter 4), and forests (Chapter 5). The case of southern Africa is notable: there the market is already generating powerful incentives for conservation. Currently about 18 percent of the land area of southern Africa is dedicated to conservation, and this amount is growing as a result of market forces and the financial incentives that they generate. It seems no exaggeration to say that we are well en route to a success story here: these developments have brought about a radical improvement in the positions of many previously endangered species in southern Africa. One of the most attractive and fascinating aspects of this development is that no governmental or international agency planned it—it happened of its own accord and without any large-scale prompting. This exemplifies the idea that the market operates in a decentralized fashion: there is no need for a central project manager or coordinator. Market forces generate incentives, and incentives move people and companies.

Africa may be rather unique in the extent of financial incentives it has offered for conservation, mainly because of its charismatic and unique fauna. However, there are encouraging examples of eco-tourism providing conservation incentives elsewhere in the world, though at this stage it is probably too early to see how important they will ultimately become. But if ecotourism and market forces only conserve the unique fauna of the African savannas, they will have accomplished a great deal of lasting value.

A word of caution is appropriate here: ecotourism has great potential for good, but mass tourism also has the potential to destroy the very ecosystems that tourists so much value. Even tourism sensi-tive to the need not to disturb local ecosystems and patterns of ani-mal behavior can have an impact on both. Wild animals in many of the more heavily visited regions of Africa are already habituated to jeeps carrying tourists, and a recent BBC-TV program showed chee-tahs using Land Rovers full of tourists as cover while stalking their prey. Many other examples can be cited.

Economic incentives are also powerful in the case of watersheds and are beginning to operate here as well. To date the main impacts have been in the United States and have been considerable. There is great potential for these forces to operate in developing countries, where they could act to conserve many areas of biological impor-tance and uniqueness. This is currently only a potential, and realiz-ing it must be a matter of great concern. We need an example like the New York watershed case in a major developing country. It should be a priority of international development and environmental agen-cies to ensure that this happens.

In the case of forests the potential is as great as in the other cases, but it remains less realized. Forests play a major role in the global carbon cycle. Conserving them prevents the release of carbon into the atmosphere, and regrowing them or allowing them to continue growing absorbs carbon from the atmosphere. Forests are an impor-tant global public good. Paying for the provision of this global pub-lic good makes eminent sense from an economic point of view. We really cannot expect it to be provided as an act of charity, especially as the countries mainly responsible for providing it are among the poorest in the world. Chapter 5 demonstrated that they are probably subsidizing the industrial countries in the provision of carbon sequestration by an amount generally comparable to the subsidies provided by industrial nations through foreign aid. Indeed, given that much foreign aid is tied to the purchase of goods from the donor country, often arms, the balance of real subsidies may be flowing from poor to rich. This is clearly a ridiculous situation, and one that we need to remedy.

As noted in Chapter 5, the Kyoto Protocol of the United Nations Framework Convention on Climate Change could introduce measures that would go far to fixing this problem. This is a powerful reason for supporting the protocol. There is already a small market in carbon sequestration resulting from the joint implementation projects initiated between industrial and developing countries. These are projects in which industrial countries, or carbon-emitting corporations in industrial countries, pay for carbon sequestration or the reduction of carbon emissions in developing countries. As an example, several electric utilities in the United States have paid for reforestation in countries in Central and South America (Schwartze 1999).

If—and this is clearly a massive *if*—we were able to realize the potential of market forces in the areas of ecotourism, watersheds, and forests, then the global impact would be truly far-reaching. We would revolutionize human interactions with our planet and make a tremendous step toward the conservation of vital planetary systems. We would contribute to improving human health, stabilizing the carbon and hydrological cycles, and conserving biodiversity.

The importance of setting up positive economic incentives for conservation simply cannot be overemphasized. Almost every day we see news reports of poor people in tropical countries who, when asked why they are burning forests and dynamiting coral reefs reply, "It's the only way we have of feeding our families." Probably they are telling the truth: it is up to those of us who want these systems conserved to ensure that the local population can earn an income from them without destroying them. If we can get the economic incentives right, there should be much less conflict between conservation and economic progress.

What is the role of biodiversity, the diversity of species and organisms, in our planetary life-support systems? In part biodiversity is a prerequisite for the functioning of many natural ecosystems. Biodiversity also improves the productivity and increases the resilience of natural systems. It makes them better able to withstand natural climatic fluctuations and changes in their environment resulting from human actions. Biodiversity also provides insurance against catastrophe and is a source of knowledge. In both roles it has been of almost unlimited value to human beings. Biodiversity provides us with a reservoir of genetic variants that can be used in the event of epidemics among the animals and crops that we cultivate for food; and it is a source of new cultivars and of enhanced productivity for existing cultivars. Indeed, all of our present agricultural practices owe their productivity to biodiversity (Council for Agricultural Science and Technology 1999).

Biodiversity is of great importance to us, yet it is in many respects a public good, so that the returns to a provider or conserver do not fully reflect the social value of its provision. In particular, in its insurance role biodiversity is a public good, and this has also traditionally been true of its role as a source of knowledge. This may alter as a result of developments in intellectual property rights legislation and international agreements such as the Kyoto Protocol and the United Nations Convention on Biodiversity. We expect that in general a market system will underprovide and underconserve biodiversity. Chapter 6 provided many examples of this. But there are some situations where biodiversity has nevertheless substantial market value. The diversity of the fauna of southern African savannas is a good case. Another is provided by the value of biodiversity as the raw material for bioprospecting. We saw in Chapter 6 that there is clearly some commercial value here but that to date it has yielded only limited returns for countries that have large reserves of biodiversity. At this point, predicting whether bioprospecting has the potential to generate important economic incentives for biodiversity conservation is difficult.

There are many cases in which the straightforward application of markets does not seem likely to lead to strong incentives for conservation of key ecosystems. Many of these are cases in which the ecosystem provides a public good whose social value cannot readily be appropriated by the provider. Some of the services of biodiversity illustrate well cases in which the unaided market systems fails to provide appropriate conservation incentives. There are, however, other economic policies and institutions that can be used in such cases. The instinctive reaction of policymakers is usually to formulate a command-and-control approach to regulation, passing laws specifically prohibiting or requiring an action. In general these are the least desirable approaches from an economic perspective: anything involving some element of market forces is usually to be preferred to a straightforward command-and-control mechanism, because these provide incentives that are positive from a business perspective. In this context, tradable permit systems have many attractions. They combine regulation—the requirement to obtain a permit before a natural resource can be used—with a market that generates incentives for reducing the costs of cutting back on the regulated activity. The regulation of sulfur dioxide emissions in the United States operates in this way. Firms need a permit to emit sulfur dioxide into the atmosphere, and the tradability of these permits means that everyone has an incentive to reduce their emission of sulfur dioxide and so sell more permits or buy fewer.

Mitigation-banking practices being adopted in conjunction with the implementation of the Endangered Species Act by the U.S. Fish and Wildlife Service provide a rather different and fascinating perspective on how such approaches can operate in other contexts. The ability to establish mitigation banks for endangered species reduces the costs of compliance with the Endangered Species Act and at the same time provides an incentive to stimulate the growth of the endangered species. There is a very strong case for rethinking many command-and-control style regulations to see whether an element of market forces and market flexibility can be introduced.

Another difficult set of issues concerns the treatment of future generations. For many, an important element in environmental conservation is leaving for future generations the natural systems and natural wealth that we inherited from the past. The extent to which this is an obligation is ultimately a matter of belief rather that something to be settled by deductive argument. There are certainly grounds for supposing that market forces will not always strike the type of balance between present and future that conservationists feel appropriate.

Back now to the main issue: the scope for using markets to manage our interactions with the natural environment. How great is this? What could it contribute? When would it work, and when would it fail? Clearly markets are already contributing in several areas and could contribute considerably more. Watersheds play economically important roles in many regions and cover a large part of the Earth's surface. Although there are no data that speak directly to this, it seems reasonable to assume that they contain a significant part of the Earth's remaining biodiversity. So conserving even 10 or 20 percent of the Earth's watersheds in pristine condition would be a major achievement. It seems likely that this would be easily justified on economic grounds. Ecotourism, as noted several times, is already responding to market forces and making a difference to the conservation prospects in southern Africa and possibly could elsewhere. Markets for carbon sequestration, while still vestigial, are emerging. They need international support to become effective. The Kyoto Protocol would provide this. There are many other ways in which markets could provide incentives for conservation: bioprospecting, mitigation banking, social purchase of environmental public goods. So the prospect of market forces contributing to planetary maintenance is certainly real and important.

Markets will never be a panacea. Too many environmental goods are public, and too many environmental problems are beyond the reach of property rights for the market to solve all of our problems. The marine environment in particular seems hard to bring within the scope of law and property rights, and as long as this continues to be the case it will be difficult to prevent the abuse of marine ecosystems. However, if we can use the market to take care of even a fraction of the interactions between human beings and their natural infrastructure, we will have freed our governmental processes and collective attention to focus on the residue of matters that cannot be solved by the more or less automatic operation of the market and that really need the attention of our political processes.

One final comment to keep matters in perspective: this book has focused on economic issues. This does not imply that these are the only or even the most important dimensions of environmental problems. There are surely complex moral and aesthetic questions associated with the way in which we treat the other species with whom we share the Earth and that are as dependent on it as we are. These raise very important questions that you may find as compelling as the economic issues dealt within this book. But you will have to look elsewhere for guidance on them!

BIBLIOGRAPHY

Aber, J. D., and J. M. Melillo. 1991. *Terrestrial Ecosystems*. Philadelphia: Saunders College Publishing.

Anderson, T. 1996. *Enviro-Capitalists: Why and How to Preserve Their Habitat*. Available from www.economics.iucn.org.

Baskin, Y. 1997. *The Work of Nature*. Washington, D.C.: Island Press.

Benedick, R. E. 1998. *Ozone Diplomacy: New Directions in Safeguarding the Planet*. Cambridge, Mass.: Harvard University Press.

Blockstein, D. 1998. "Lyme Disease and the Passenger Pigeon." *Science* 279:1831.

Bonalume, N. R., and D. Dickson. 1999. "$3M Deal Launches Major Hunt for Drug Leads in Brazil." *Nature* 400:302.

Bond, I. 1993. *The Economics of Wildlife and Landuse in Zimbabwe: An Examination of Current Knowlege and Issues*. WWF Program Office, Harare, P.O. Box CY, 1409 Causway, Zimbabwe, WWF Multispecies Animal Production Systems Project.

Botsford, L. W., J. C. Castillo, et al. 1997. "The Management of Fisheries and Marine Ecosystems." *Science* (25 July) 277:509–15.

Brander, J. A., and M. S. Taylor. 1998. "The Simple Economics of Easter Island: A Ricardo-Malthus Model of Renewable Resource Use." *American Economic Review* 88, no. 1:119–38.

Broome, J. 1992. *Counting the Cost of Global Warming*. London: White Horse Press.

Brown, G. M., Jr., and J. F. Shogren. 1998. "The Economics of the Endangered Species Act." *Journal of Economic Perspectives* 12, no. 3:3–20.

Carte, B. K. 1996. "The Biomedical Potential of Marine Natural Products." *BioScience* 46, no. 4:271–86.

Chapin, F. S. I., B. H. Walker, et al. 1997. "Biotic Control over the Functioning of Ecosystems." *Science* 277:500.

Chichilnisky, G. 1996. "An Axiomatic Approach to Sustainable Development." *Social Choice and Welfare* 13, no. 2:219–48.

———. 2000. "Ecology and the Knowledge Revolution." In *Nature and Human Society: The Quest for a Sustainable World. Proceedings of the 1997 Forum on Biodiversity,* edited by P. Raven et al. Washington, D.C.: National Academy Press.

Chichilnisky, G., and G. Heal. 1998. "Economic Returns from the Biosphere." *Nature* 391:629–30.

———. 2000. *Environmental Markets: Equity and Efficiency.* New York: Columbia University Press.

Cline, W. R. 1992. *The Economics of Global Warming.* Washington, D.C.: Institute for International Economics.

Coase, R. 1960. "The Problem of Social Cost." *Journal of Law and Economics* 3:1–44.

Cohen, J., and G. D. Tilman. 1996. "Enhanced: Biosphere 2 and Biodiversity—The Lessons So Far." *Science* 274:1150–51.

Costanza, R., R. d'Arge, et al. 1997. "The Value of the World's Ecosystem Services and Natural Resources." *Nature* 387:253–60.

Council for Agricultural Science and Technology. 1999. *The Benefits of Biodiversity.* Ames, Iowa: Committee on Agriculture Science and Technology.

Cumming, D. H. M. 1990a. *Are Multispecies Systems a Viable Landuse Option for Southern African Savannas?* Harare, Zimbabwe: WWF Multispecies Animal Production Systems Project.

———. 1990b. *Wildlife and the Marketplace: A View from Southern Africa.* Harare, Zimbabwe: WWF Multispecies Animal Production Systems Project.

Cumming, D. H. M., and I. Bond. 1991. *Animal Production in Southern Africa: Present Practices and Opportunities for Peasant Farmers in Arid Lands.* Harare, Zimbabwe: WWF Multispecies Animal Production Systems Project.

Daily, G. C., ed. 1997. *Nature's Services: Societal Dependence on Natural Ecosystems.* Washington, D.C.: Island Press.

Daily, G. C., and S. Dasgupta. 2000. "Ecosystem Services." In *Encyclopedia of Biodiversity,* edited by S. A. Levin. San Diego: Academic Press.

Daily, G. C., P. A. Matson, et al. 1997. "Ecosystem Services Supplied by Soil." In *Nature's Services: Societal Dependence on Natural Ecosystems,* edited by G. C. Daily. Washington, D.C.: Island Press.

Dasgupta, P. S., and G. M. Heal. 1979. *Economic Theory and Exhaustible Resources.* Cambridge: Cambridge University Press.

Diamond, J. 1995. "Easter's End." *Discover* (August): 63–69.

———. 1997. *Guns, Germs, and Steel.* New York and London: W. W. Norton.

Drake, J. A. 1989. *Biological Invasions: A Global Perspective*. Chichester: John Wiley & Sons.

Drinkwater, L. E., P. Wagoner, et al. 1998. "Legume-Based Cropping Systems Have Reduced Carbon and Nitrogen Losses." *Nature* 396 (19 November): 262–65.

Eckholm, E. 1998. "Stunned by Floods, China Hastens Logging Curbs." *New York Times*. 27 September.

Economist, The. 2000. "Farming in the Garden of Eden." 25 March.

Ecotourism Society, The. 1998. "Ecotourism Statistical Fact Sheet." Available from www.ecotourism.org/tocfr.html

Ehrlich, P. 1988. "The Loss of Biodiversity." In *Biodiversity*, edited by E. O. Wilson. Washington, D.C.: National Academy Press, 21–27.

Ehrlich, P., and A. Ehrlich. 1981. *Extinctions*. New York: Ballantine Books.

Ehrlich, P. R. 1997. *A World of Wounds: Ecologists and the Human Dilemma*. Oldendorf/Luhe, Germany: Ecology Institute.

Ehrlich, P. R., and P. Raven. 1964. "Butterflies and Plants: A Study in Coevolution." *Evolution* 8:586–608.

Eldridge, N. 1998. *Life in the Balance: Humanity and the Biodiversity Crisis*. Princeton, N.J.: Princeton University Press.

Epstein, P. R. 1998. *Marine Ecosystems: Emerging Diseases as Indicators of Change*. Cambridge, Mass.: Harvard Medical School, Center for Health and the Global Environment.

———. 1999. *Extreme Weather Events: The Health and Economic Consequences of the 1997/8 El Niño and La Niña*. Cambridge, Mass.: Harvard Medical School, Center for Health and the Global Environment.

Estrada-Oyeula, R. 2000. "The Kyoto Protocol." In *Environmental Markets: Equity and Efficiency*, edited by G. Chichilnisky and G. Heal. New York: Columbia University Press.

Financial Times (London). 1998. "Too Much Food." 17 November.

———. 2000. "Organic Food Prices Race Ahead." 22 March.

Foley, D. 1970. "Lindahl's Solution and the Core of an Economy with Public Goods." *Econometrica* 38(1):66–72.

Freese, C. H. 1999. *Wild Species as Commodities: Managing Markets and Ecosystems for Sustainability*. Washington, D.C.: Island Press.

Grime, J. P. 1997. "Biodiversity and Ecosystems Function: The Debate Deepens." *Science* 277:1260.

Grimes, A., P. Loomis, et al. 1994. "Valuing the Rain Forest: The Economic Value of Nontimber Forest Products in Ecuador." *Ambio* 23:405–10.

Grubb, M., and D. Brack. 1999. *The Kyoto Protocol: A Guide and Assessment*. London: Royal Institute of International Affairs.

Harrod, R. 1948. *Towards A Dynamic Economics*. London: Macmillan.

Heal, G. 1998. *Valuing the Future: Economic Theory and Sustainability*. New York: Columbia University Press.

Heal, G. M., and G. Chichilnisky. 1991. *Oil in the International Economy*. Oxford: Oxford University Press.

Honey, M. 1999. *Ecotourism and Sustainable Development: Who Owns Paradise?* Washington, D.C.: Island Press.

Hooper, D. U., and P. M. Vitousek. 1997. "The Effect of Plant Composition and Diversity on Ecosystem Processes." *Science* 277:1302–5.

Houghton, J. J., L. G. Filho, et al. 1996. *Climate Change 1995: The Science of Climate Change.* Cambridge: Cambridge University Press.

Hughes, J., G. C. Daily, et al. 1997. "Population Diversity: Its Extent and Extinction." *Science* 278 (24 October): 689–92.

Independent, The. 2000. "Nearly One in Three Now Eats Organic Products." 8 February.

Jorling, T. C. 1999. "Incentive-Based Management Strategies: A 'Common-Sense' Approach to Conservation of Biological Diversity." *The Science of the Total Environment* 240.

Kats, G., S. Kumar, et al. 1999. "The Role for an International Measurement and Verification Standard in Reducing Pollution." Paper presented at ECEE Summer Study, Energy Efficiency and CO_2 Reduction: The Dimensions of the Social Challenge, 31 May–4 June, Menedlieu, France.

Kerr, R. A. 1998. "Acid Rain Control: Success on the Cheap." *Science* 282 (6 November): 1024.

Kremen, C., J. Niles, et al. 1999. *Economics of Forest Conservation Across Scales.* Palo Alto, Calif.: Center for Conservation Biology, Stanford University.

———. 2000. "Economic Incentives for Rain Forest Conservation Across Scales." *Science* 288 (9 June): 1828–32.

Lanza, A., and F. Pigliaru. 1999. *Why Are Tourism Countries Small and Fast-Growing?* Paris: International Energy Agency.

Lowenstein, G., and J. Elster, eds. 1992. *Choice over Time.* New York: Russell Sage Foundation.

Lubchenco, J. 1998. "Entering the Century of the Environment." *Science* 279:491–98.

Mankiw, N. G. 1997. *Principles of Economics.* New York: The Dryden Press.

Matson, P. A., W. J. Parton, et al. 1997. "Agricultural Intensification and Ecosystem Properties." *Science* 277 (25 July): 504–9.

McGrady-Steed, J., P. M. Harris, et al. 1997. "Biodiversity Regulates Ecosystem Predictability." *Nature* 390:162–65.

McMichael, A. 1993. *Planetary Overload: Globlal Environmental Change and the Health of the Human Species.* Cambridge: Cambridge University Press.

Morell, V. 1997. "Antiobiotic Resistance: Road of No Return." *Science* 278 (24 October): 575–76.

Myers, N. 1997. "Biodiversity's Genetic Library." In *Nature's Services: Societal Dependence on Natural Ecosystems,* edited by G. C. Daily. Washington, D.C.: Island Press.

Nabhan, G. P., and S. Buchmann. 1996. *Forgotten Pollinators*. Washington, D.C.: Island Press.

———. 1997. "Services Provided by Pollinators." In *Nature's Services: Societal Dependence on Natural Ecosystems,* edited by G. C. Daily. Washington, D.C.: Island Press.

Naeem, G. F., and S. Li. 1997. "Biodiversity Enhances Ecosystem Reliability." *Nature* 390:505–9.

National Research Council. 1999. *A Framework for Managing Biodiversity: Report of the Committee on the Economic and Non-Economic Value of Biodiversity.* Washington, D.C.: National Research Council.

Nature. 1998. "When Rhetoric Hits Reality in the Debate on Bioprospecting." 392:535–40.

———. 1999. "Monsanto Concession on Engineered Corn." *Nature* 397:98.

Naylor, R., and P. R. Ehrlich. 1997. "Natural Pest Control Services in Agriculture." In *Nature's Services: Societal Dependence on Natural Ecosystems,* edited by G. C. Daily. Washington, D.C.: Island Press.

Parker, R. 1994. *The Common Stream.* Chicago: Academy Chicago Publishers.

Perfecto, I., R. A. Rice, et al. 1996. "Shade Coffee: A Disappearing Refuge for Biodiversity." *BioScience* 46, no. 8:598–608.

Pigou, A. C. 1932. *The Economics of Welfare.* London: Macmillan.

Postel, S., and S. Carpenter. 1997. "Freshwater Ecosystem Services." In *Nature's Services: Societal Dependence on Natural Ecosystems,* edited by G. C. Daily. Washington, D.C.: Island Press.

Postel, S. L., G. C. Daily, et al. 1996. "Human Appropriation of Renewable Fresh Water." *Science* 271:785–88.

Power, M. E., G. D. Tilman, et al. 1996. "Challenges in the Quest for Keystone Species." *BioScience* 46, no. 8:609–20.

Ramsey, F. P. 1928. "A Mathematical Theory of Saving." *Economic Journal* 38:543–59.

Rausser, G. C. and A. A. Small. 2000. "Valuing Research Leads: Bioprospecting and the Conservation of Genetic Resources." *Journal of Political Economy* (February).

Read, D. 1998. "Plants on the Web." *Nature* 396.

Reid, W. V. 1998. "A Business Plan for Ecosystem Services: Extending the New York City Watershed Model to Other Geographic Regions and Other Ecosystem Services." In *Managing Human-Dominated Ecosystems,* edited by P. Raven. St. Louis: Missouri Botanical Gardens.

Reid, W. V., S. A. Laird, et al. 1993. *Biodiversity Prospecting: Using Genetic Resources for Sustainable Development.* Washington, D.C.: World Resources Institute.

Revenga, C., S. Murray, et al. 1998. *Watersheds of the World.* Washington, D.C.: World Resources Institute and Worldwatch Institute.

Ricardo, D. 1911. *Principles of Political Economy and Taxation.* London: Everyman's Library.

Rubenstein, D. I. 1993. "Science and the Pursuit of a Sustainable World." *Ecological Applications* 3:585–87.

Schwartze, R. 1999. *Activities Implemented Jointly: Another Look at the Facts.* Palo Alto, Calif.: Center for Environmental Science and Policy, Stanford University.

Simpson, R. D., R. A. Sedjo, et al. 1996. "Valuing Biodiversity for Use in Pharmaceutical Research." *Quarterly Journal of Economics* 104, no. 1:163–85.

Sinclair, A. R. E. 1979. *Serengeti: Dynamics of an Ecosystem.* Chicago: University of Chicago Press.

Sinclair, M. T. 1998. "Tourism and Economic Development: A Survey." *Journal of Development Studies* 34:1–51.

Skiddelsky, R. 1992. *John Maynard Keynes: The Economist as Savior, 1920–1937.* London and New York: Penguin Books.

Smith, A. 1977. *An Inquiry into the Nature and Causes of the Wealth of Nations.* Chicago: University of Chicago Press.

Stierle, A., G. Stroble, et al. 1993. "Taxol and Taxane Production by *Taxomyces andreanae,* and Endophytic Fungus of Pacific Yew." *Science* 260 (9 April): 214–16.

Thies, C., and T. Tscharntke. 1999. "Landscape Structure and Biological Control in Agroecosystems." *Science* 285, no. 5429:893–985.

Tietenberg, T. 1992. *Environmental and Natural Resource Economics.* New York: Harper Collins.

Tilman, D. 1998. "The Greening of the Green Revolution." *Nature* 396:211–12.

Tilman, D., and J. A. Downing. 1994. "Biodiversity and Stability in Grasslands." *Nature* 367:363–65.

Tilman, D., S. Naeem, et al. 1997. "Biodiversity and Ecosystem Properties." *Science* 278:1866–67.

Toman, M. A. 1998. "Why Not Calculate the Value of the World's Ecosystem Services and Natural Capital." *Ecological Economics* 25:57–60.

Trust for Public Lands. 1997. *Protecting the Source: Land Conservation and the Future of America's Drinking Water.* San Francisco: The Trust for Public Lands.

United Nations Environment Program. 1999. *Unsafe Water: 3.3 Billion Illnesses and 5.3 Million Deaths.* New York: United Nations Environment Program.

U.S. Department of Agriculture. 1997. *Agricultural Handbook Number 712, Agricultural Resources and Environmental Indicators 1996–97.* Washington, D.C.: U.S. Department of Agriculture, 286–96.

Van der Heijden, M. G. A., J. N. Klironomos, et al. 1998. "Mycorrhizal Fungal Diversity Determines Plant Biodiversity, Ecosystem Variability and Productivity." *Nature* 396:69–71.

Vitousek, P. M., H. A. Mooney, et al. 1997. "Human Domination of Earth's Ecosystems." *Science* 277:494–99.

Wilson, E. O., ed. 1988. *Biodiversity.* Washington, D.C.: National Academy Press.

———. 1993. *The Diversity of Life.* Cambridge, Mass.: Harvard University Press.

———. 1998. *Consilience.* New York: Alfred A. Knopf.

Witte, W. 1998. "Medical Consequences of Antibiotic Use in Agriculture." *Science* 279 (13 February): 996–97.

World Bank. 1998. *Promoting Forest Conservation and Management by Creating Markets for Forest Services.* Washington, D.C.: The World Bank.

Index

195